Wendy Salisbury was born in London in 1946, descended from Russian-Jewish immigrants. Alongside her passionate private life, she is a writer, an antique dealer, an events organizer and a very Noughties grandmother.

THE TOYBOY DIARIES 2

The Daily Male

WENDY SALISBURY

Old St PUBLISHING

First published in 2009 by Old Street Publishing Ltd

40 Bowling Green Lane, London EC1R 0BJ

www.oldstreetpublishing.co.uk

ISBN 978-1-906964-02-3

10 9 8 7 6 5 4 3 2 1

A CIP catalogue record for this title is available from the British Library.

Typeset by Martin Worthington.

Printed and bound in Great Britain.

We enter the world alone and we leave it alone . . . and in the middle, we owe it to ourselves to find a little company.

Meredith Grey, 'Grey's Anatomy'

*I dedicate this book to every man and woman looking for love.
If you find it, cherish it! If you don't, keep looking . . .*

FOREPLAY

When I finished writing my first book, *The Toyboy Diaries*, on my 60th birthday in 2006, some people said I should quit while I was ahead. Whether they meant writing or researching, I'm not sure – but how could I quit when there was still 'research' about which to write? And so I became a blogger . . .

The blog that turned into this book has changed shape many times. Whenever an unsuspecting manboy crossed my path, he'd be shoehorned neatly into the next chapter. Some objected so they were removed; some didn't ring the chemistry bell so they were expelled; and those who hoped to be included had some stringent tests to pass! Without exception, they provided entertainment of one sort or another . . .

While my first volume of memoirs may have shocked – that would be the sex on every four pages – this story is more considered. Don't get me wrong: I'd still love to have sex 'every four pages', or at least every four weeks; but although the option is there, I seem to be growing up (that's UP, not OLD!) and have become a little more selective. And despite signs to the contrary, I would still enjoy a complete relationship with a perfect and suitable man, if only God had created one!

It is apparent that the vast majority of older single women are searching for this mythical Right Man: a charming, chivalrous, well-preserved, financially secure older gentleman with whom to spend their autumn years. I occasionally polish my quiver and join in the hunt, but when night falls over the Serengeti (or in my case Paddington Recreation Ground), I still prefer the insecure, inappropriate, inconsistent attentions of a fit young buck. Go figure!

Older women's lives are, thankfully, changing with the speed at which the 'Send Message' button can be pressed on an internet-dating website. We are less invisible now, more respected. Society and the media are finally acknowledging that the sophisticated siren has her own story to tell – and a fascinating one it is too.

The great French novelist Flaubert put it best of all, describing the older woman's life as: 'A period which combines reflection and tenderness, when maturity kindles a warmer flame in the eye, when strength of heart mingles with experience of life, and when, in the fullness of its development, the whole being overflows with a wealth of harmony and beauty.'

Well said, Gustave! I'll drink to that.

Although men still show signs of wanting women to be their cook, housekeeper, nursemaid, ironing bored (sic) and sex slave, they remain the cream in our coffee, the lace on our lingerie and the budding new shoots in our winter gardens.

Without them, this memoir would not have been written, so thank you all – even those who loved me and left me – for passing through my life and making it a more interesting place.

One

You can't go on shagging 28-year-olds forever! Where do you think you'll be in five years time?'

'Shagging 33-year olds?' I answer hopefully.

Calm Best Friend (CBF) looks at me disapprovingly over the top of her half-moon specs and purses her lips. Although I'm three years her senior, I feel like a wayward schoolgirl.

This discussion has arisen because following twenty-two years of dating younger men, the Sisterhood is on a mission to see me settled, once and for all, with an *older* man. Calm, in her capacity as spokeswoman, has been chosen to put the screws on – and they're not the kind of screws I generally enjoy.

I usually run my problems past CBF because she's the least judgmental person I know. A great listener and advisor, she may suggest an alternative mode of behaviour but she rarely tells me I'm actually wrong. This, in my opinion, is a great quality in a friend. Since qualifying as a Life Coach, however, she is more determined than ever to steer people towards *achieving their attainable goals with clarity and confidence while removing real or perceived barriers.*

Random bed-hopping with guys young enough to be my plumber obviously falls foul of this particular remit.

'Darling,' she scolds, trying to frown though the Botox won't let her. 'You've got to start acting your age, not your bra size. You may think you're still fit and fabulous – and of course, you are – but now you've joined the bus-pass brigade your toyboy days are numbered. It's time to get sensible. You don't want to end up . . . '

'*Lonely in my old age*?' I parrot at her. 'That's what my mother said when I divorced for the first time and what my daughters said when I divorced for the second!'

'Well you have to agree – they had a point.'

Our food arrives and CBF slides her fork into her Penne Puttanesca. I swirl mine around in my Carbonara but find the flavour sadly lacking. I catch the waiter's eye and indicate that I would like some extra seasoning. He strides across the floor brandishing a giant pepper mill that he grinds atop my pasta until I raise my hand for him to stop. I smile in thanks and bat my eyelashes at him because he's young and he's cute and . . .

'Have you developed a tic or something?' CBF interrupts. 'And have you listened to a word I've said?'

'No. I mean, yes. Of course I have, but come on! Don't tell me you'd object to *that* being washed and brought to your tent?'

She shakes her head despairingly but there's a glint in her eye. She knows the score, even if it doesn't tally. She too has drunk from the fountain of youth and found the taste intoxicating, yet she's determined to have this forthright talk and won't give up that easily.

'You're in danger of embarrassing yourself,' she goes on, kindly but firmly. 'Do I need to remind you you'll be 62 next birthday? It's time to stop this toyboy nonsense and find someone appropriate before it's too late.'

I roll my eye skywards and leap to my own defense. 'I've

been out with loads of older men! Suitable suitors press their suit on me with mind-numbing regularity. Mind you, some of their suits truly do need pressing. Older men don't always know where their local dry cleaners are . . . but the main problem is: *they just don't turn me on*! Anyway, where is it written that how I live is wrong? Did you know that in some cultures the mating of older women with younger men is actively encouraged? Pubescent boys visit the female elders to lose their virginity and learn about procreation. Well I've done procreation and now I want recreation! And I'm not going to find that with some grizzled old has-been.'

'What about Arnold?' CBF suggests in the sort of voice reserved for an elderly relative when a Care Home is the final solution. 'He still looks good for his age. And he's quite lively, isn't he? He climbed Everest last year. And you like him, don't you?'

'It was a gentle trek in the foothills, actually, not a vertical assault on the north peak. And of course I like him – he's a sweetheart – but I don't like him *like that*. His face fits at the Royal Opera House or on the first tee at Gleneagles, but between my tawny thighs? I don't think so.'

CBF sighs and takes my hand.

'Look darling,' she reasons, 'we . . . I mean, *I* have only got your best interests at heart. There are so many charming, decent older men out there – you'd have much more in common with one of them. And a man like that would take care of you unlike these . . . these *juveniles* you insist on collecting like butterflies on a board.'

'Would I could pin them down for that long,' I mumble wistfully and contrive to change the subject.

We talk about her new career, catch up on the gossip about family and friends, discuss ways to boost our income in the shaky economy and linger on the current main event in my life: my younger daughter's forthcoming wedding.

'Who are you taking?' CBF asks, tilting her head enquiringly.

'I'm not sure,' I reply slowly. 'I've no one really suitable. I may have to fly solo on this one. You're lucky to have Maurice, you know . . .' Too late, I realize I've tumbled into her trap. I can hear her thinking *I rest your case* even though her lips don't move.

Most of my single friends are in relationships but I am currently in 'no man land' – or at least 'no man I could introduce to my family' land. I'd obviously prefer to be properly partnered on such an auspicious occasion but as I'm unlikely to meet Suitable Sam this side of the wedding, I've invited a few male mates along to ensure I don't have to dance the night away in the bingo-winged clutches of Aunt Miriam – or worse still, find myself sitting alone like a complete saddo.

I reflect on the fact that I was also on my own at my elder daughter Poppy's wedding thirteen years ago (unless you count a brief fling with one of the groom's friends, before, during and after that event).

In my head I know CBF is right, but in my heart I suppress a little shudder. I haven't fancied an older man since Charlton Heston came down from Mount Sinai carrying *The Ten Commandments*, for what older man could give me the electrical charge I feel when I'm with a hot young stud?

We finish our pasta and CBF, on an eternal diet, declines dessert. The moment of introspection has drained my blood-sugar level though, and I am now in urgent need of medical intervention in the shape of a large slice of Chocolate Cherry Cheesecake. The sugar rush restores my glucose balance and I return to the argument, batteries recharged.

'You remember that last date I had with Jerry Atrick?' I ask, speaking his name in inverted commas. 'He spent the entire evening talking about his prostate. It was so excruciating I wanted to drown in my soup.'

CBF thinks for a moment. 'Are you talking about Roger?' she asks. 'You make him sound about 92. He's only 65!'

'Is he really?' I reply sardonically. 'You could have fooled me . . .'

'They're not *all* like that,' CBF forges on, absent-mindedly helping herself to a large forkful of my creamy cake. 'There are plenty of healthy ones around. You've just got to open your mind to them. Give them a chance. I don't want you to self-destruct, that's all.'

'I know,' I concede. 'And I appreciate that you – and whoever's put you up to this – care about my future wellbeing. The thing is, sweetie, my lifestyle doesn't harm anyone. Except me, occasionally, but that's my choice.'

She opens her mouth to protest so I hurry on. 'I do hear what you're saying though . . .'

'And you promise you'll try and mend your wicked ways?'

This criticism jars. Up to now, I've thoroughly enjoyed my wicked ways. 'I'll try,' I say cautiously, not entirely convinced, 'but it's not as if I go out trawling for them – they come to me! You'd be amazed at how many young men want the *older woman experience*. They'd much rather date a sophisticated lady than a "ladette" any day.'

CBF still looks doubtful. This time it's me who reaches over and pats her hand. 'OK. *I promise!*' I say, and we pay the bill, kiss goodbye and agree, as always, to talk tomorrow.

♀

I ponder CBF's advice as I drive home. Maybe she does have a point. Maybe I should stop listening exclusively to my own advice and pay attention to someone else's for a change – especially, as has been proven, I'm not always right. I am growing older, although I don't feel it, and Arnold or someone of his ilk might not be so bad. Arnold's nice enough: tallish, slimmish, Jewish, erudite, presentable, cultured, rich. Being with him would remove some of the aggravation from my life, but what would it *add* exactly – apart from a fully staffed house, five-star holidays, designer shopping sprees, fine wining and dining, and financial security? Oh all right, these are all attractive attributes I'll admit – but what about The Danger! The Excitement! The Adventure! These are the highs I've courted for so long.

I slam on the brakes as a reckless young courier zigzags in front of me. I'm not ready to die yet even if it is with a fit biker's helmet in my lap. I blast my horn, admire his leather-clad ass disappearing into the distance and return to mulling over CBF's suggestion.

If I'm honest, I'll admit that some of my recent adventures have been as fleeting as a summer's day and twice as poignant. There was that suave French guy I met at the art auction. The registration desk had run out of catalogues so I let him share mine. We sat with our heads together for about an hour until he'd completed his bids, then he asked if I fancied a coffee. The coffee turned into drinks; the drinks became dinner. Later that night I invited him back to my flat to value some limited-editions prints I wanted to sell and we ended up downing a bottle of champagne and having sex on the sofa. I left the auction without any art, but what an artist he turned out to be!

Then there was the bookish young chap I used to nod to occasionally in the local café where I write. I was having problems with my laptop one morning and he heard me tutting and asked if he could help. His hand brushed mine as he took over the keyboard and a charge ran through me like a lightning bolt. He was in the café every day after that and we struck up a flirty kind of friendship. One evening, when I was packing up, he asked me if I fancied some sushi. We went for a Japanese meal and after a few cups of saki, he admitted he really fancied me. I was secretly delighted but managed to keep my cool.

Then one sweltering afternoon, not long after, I was in the café struggling with an article on whether the Six-Date Rule still applies in today's 'must-have' society. Bookish and I were having a major eye-fuck and I just thought – I want him now! I was hot and restless, so I told him I was popping home *for a cold shower*. He picked up the euphemism and got up and followed me. We fell on each other as soon as we walked in my door. Talk about afternoon delight!

The situation was fun while it lasted but it lasted a little longer than it was fun. He kept turning up on my doorstep uninvited with stupid excuses like his hot water had been cut off so could he please use mine, and I stopped going to the café after that in order to avoid him. Some flings do have a short but sweet shelf life . . .

I park the car outside my flat still pondering the implications of the lunch conversation. At least with an Arnold I might find a companion who would satisfy my friends and family and become a more permanent fixture in my life. And while I'm listing the positives, I wouldn't have to explain who Muffin the Mule was, or about pounds, shillings and pence. And the fact that I saw the Beatles live. Twice!

There would be a shared history to draw on because although most young men find my stories fascinating, we come from very different eras. I was born in 1946 and my childhood memories recall London as a drab and sepia place, all post-war gloom and freezing school mornings. I had to get dressed in the dead of winter in front of a one-bar electric fire; no wussy central heating for the likes of us!

Look after your pennies and your pounds will look after you cautioned my grandmother, so I learned to be frugal and strong from a stalwart woman who was widowed at 29 with two children to support.

Come and help me change this fuse coaxed my father, who'd been desperate for a son and often treated me as one. (Learning to 'change this fuse' has stood me in good stead all my life.)

Sew this hem by hand taught my mother, a dress designer who trained in Paris in the 1930s and instilled in me a hungry creativity and a love of elegant clothes.

Both sets of grandparents had been Russian-Jewish immigrants who'd escaped persecution from the Cossacks in the 1880s. They'd suffered extraordinary hardship and deprivation, but despite this, they were resilient refugees determined to improve their lot.

Soon after I was born, my family set sail for the New World – the United States of America! We returned to London four years later though because my mother was homesick, and having nowhere to live, we moved in with my maternal grandmother and her second husband. London was still reeling from the fall-out of WWII and I can remember going shopping with Gaga, as

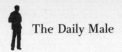

we used to call her, and having to use ration books. She'd tear off the little coupons: one for butter, one for milk, another for some meat or a piece of cheese.

Fast-forward to 1988, and you'd have found me two marriages, two daughters and two rather unpleasant divorces later, a newly single woman of 42 beginning to live her life back to front. I hadn't dated much before I got married so I threw myself headlong into my newly single status. Then, on a ski trip to the Alps, I was seduced by my first toyboy, aged 19, and the rest, as they say, is 'her story' . . .

I let myself into my flat and kick off my shoes. I check my messages and emails, return a couple of phone calls and business enquiries, let my daughters know I'm home in case they need me and make sure there's something in the fridge for supper. Like most women, I assume many roles: a mother to my children, a daughter to my mother, an indulger to my grandchildren, a listener to my friends, an antiques dealer, an aspiring writer, an *experienced older woman* to any young man who crosses my path. I enjoy these multi-personae but I occasionally wonder: which one of them is the real me?

Maybe it is time to travel another route, I think to myself later as I pull out the ironing board and settle down for an industrious evening in front of the telly. A more sedate and settled life could be the way forward. It might be a relief to get up in the morning and slip into some comfi-fit slacks and a floral blouse instead of squeezing my *derrière* into a pair of skinny jeans and my boobs into the latest Wonderbra.

I could join a cake decorating class; indulge in a little light basket weaving. Would that be so terrible? The prospect of stability

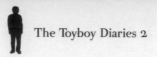

and security seem rather attractive and I feel my shoulders relax as I slide the iron to and fro across my freshly laundered, Egyptian-cotton sheets. God knows, I've courted craziness for long enough and it hasn't always made me happy. I dampen a pink linen shirt and begin to press it thoughtfully.

'An older man?' I say out loud. 'Only one way to find out.'

Two

I awake the next morning in something of a quandary. I've never been what you'd call virtuous, and as for *growing old gracefully*, that's not a club I thought I'd subscribe to. I do however feel duty bound to keep my promise to Calm Best Friend so I decide to give her suggestion a try. I switch the radio from Virgin to Woman's Hour and listen attentively to a discussion about the demise of the bone-china dinner service. I normally do a workout to some rock music at this time of day but Wendy *Nouvelle* might not need to do that any more. An oasis of sweets, puddings and cakes dances temptingly before me. What bliss to eat what I want and let it all hang out! An older man won't mind the extra poundage, will he?

People often ask me how I dare take my clothes off in front of a 25-year-old at my age, but I've never had a problem with it. I only undress in the softest of lighting and by the time we've got to that stage, the only eye he's looking out of is the one at the end of his one-eyed snake. And it might surprise you to know that younger men don't mind the subtle depreciation of a more mature body – they appreciate the womanly package as part of the experience. Anodyne flawlessness of the cover girl variety lacks the character that real women have in spades and not one man I know would rather bed a size 0 than a size 12 or 14. They like something to get their teeth into!

Nevertheless I do look after myself with carb control, yoga and Pilates, and I often go on what I call a 'half-diet' – I eat everything I want, but I only eat half of it, so: only one spoonful of sugar in my tea, only one chocolate biscuit, only one glass of wine, and white food only once a week and never after 6 p.m. (that's bread, potatoes, pasta and rice – all those lovely doughy things that have little nutritional value and settle round your middle like tyres round the Michelin man). Yes, it's a discipline but it's worth it: discipline is character building.

Of course, my regime of horizontal exercise has also helped to keep me slim. If I comply with Calm's suggestion and eschew my shenanigans to begin a more prudent life, I'll have to find some other means of exertion to stay in shape. Hill walking perhaps, or high-energy macramé, neither of which have quite the same appeal . . .

I enter my walk-in wardrobe and scour the rails for something elegant to wear. Not being the owner of a tweed skirt nor a twin set (although I have occasionally being on the receiving end of a pearl necklace) I settle on a pair of navy trousers and a cream cashmere V-neck. I apply my make-up a little more lightly than usual, omitting the second coat of mascara and the shimmery blusher to enhance my cheekbones.

I stand back and contemplate myself in the mirror. I see a slim, middle-aged woman, still attractive, but lacking a certain *je ne sais quoi*. I'm not convinced it's really me. I normally wear something a little sexier during the day (and by night, a rubber Cat Woman outfit complete with whiskers and thigh-length boots. Not every evening of course, just now and then.) I take

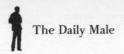

another look at myself, shrug uncertainly and head down the hall to the office.

I work through the morning on a new chapter for my book on future collectibles. I'm hoping to educate a generation brought up on disposability to select and treasure possessions longer than they would a Pret A Manger sandwich. Thanks to the plethora of TV programmes, most people know a little about mainstream art and antiques. Watching the 'Antiques Road-show' on a Sunday evening or rummaging through car-boot sales in the hope of finding that priceless Fabergé egg or unique Lalique vase are national pastimes. But I'm looking to a new market: the thirty-something city boys who (used to) get huge bonuses and want something new and original to invest in.

I've written chapters on contemporary African Art (yet to be exploited) and how to acquire your own Polynesian island (then rent it out to friends). I'm also researching the collectability of the Acabion, a limited-edition sports car super bike. The plan is to write fifty chapters but I'd like to pen a hundred – this is an endlessly fascinating subject to a person as curious as me.

Growing up near Notting Hill, I used to spend most Saturday mornings exploring the stalls of Portobello Market. I love the touch, smell and feel of beautiful old things (inanimate ones, at any rate) and have often wished they could come to life and tell me their stories. Occasionally I get lucky, and a Victorian writing-slope will reveal an ancient, faded *billet doux* hidden in a secret drawer. Antiques are so evocative and romantic – conjuring up a gentler time of days gone by. I do, however, prefer them aesthetically placed around my flat rather than knocking persistently on my bedroom door.

♀

I become totally absorbed in my writing and jump when I hear the bell ring at 6.30 p.m. It's my daughter, Lily, on her way home from work, popping round to show me the proofs for her wedding invitations. She kisses me hello on both cheeks then looks me up and down. She frowns uncomprehendingly as she takes in the sober outfit.

'You OK, Mum?' she asks. 'Anyone died?'

'No,' I answer primly. 'I'm allowed to look smart, aren't I?'

'Smart's one thing, but frumpy? It's not your usual style.'

I take note. My efforts at mature sophistication have been dismissed with a handful of carelessly chosen words.

She unpacks a fat envelope and spreads the proofs out neatly on the kitchen table. She's found an online company that produces stylish modern designs for a quarter of the price of a Smythson stiffie. I'm all for saving a few bob – why are weddings soooo expensive? – so I 'ooh!' and 'aah!' enthusiastically as we leaf through them.

We narrow the choice down to a cream and bronze 8" x 4" and an écru and silver 6" x 6". She wants to run them past her fiancé before making the final decision. The wording is another issue: although her father and I still have the same surname, we can't put them together as in *Mr and Mrs*. It would make us sound as if we were still married.

'You will have a dance with Daddy, won't you?' Lily asks as I hand her a cup of tea. 'For old times' sake?' Her pretty face looks slightly anxious so I nod reassuringly. My ex-husband and I get on well. The reasons we split up no longer apply, but he still loves his golf and I still love my freedom.

'Oh!' she says suddenly, 'and who are you bringing? Not an unsuitable, I hope!'

'Yes, darling, I wanted to broach that with you,' I say seriously. 'The other night I met the most divine young man – he's a bricklayer I picked up on a building site. He's sixteen so it's all quite legal, and he should scrub up nicely once I've taken him shopping in Milan.' I smile innocently. 'That'll be OK, won't it?'

Lily narrows her eyes and pulls a *don't-you-dare* face at me. I keep mine straight for a second or two then burst out laughing. She may have developed bride-brain but at least she hasn't become Bridezilla. All she wants is for her day to be perfect, and I can't deny her that.

'Not only am I *not* bringing an "unsuitable", but I'm actually thinking of – no – I've actually *decided* to try to walk the straight and narrow. Peer pressure has finally got to me. It's been suggested I give up toyboys for good.'

She looks at me doubtfully this time. 'Really?' she says after a moment. 'What brought this on? Mind you, it's about time you came to your senses. Your . . . um . . . *social* life's been a source of embarrassment for Poppy and me for way too long.'

I'm afraid this is true. From the point of view of their kids, mothers should be seen and not heard – and definitely not heard talking on the radio about having sex with Much Younger Men. My daughters do, however, know that I will always be there for them. And I try to strike a balance between being a good mum and having some fun without doing anything too cringe-worthy.

Lily is eyeing me curiously. 'Have you actually met someone?' she asks.

'Well . . . not exactly – but I'm hoping to. There's a man in the pipeline my friends think might be nice . . . '

She nods vaguely and, with that, the finer points of my future are hastily dismissed. I note my own use of the word *nice* to describe Arnold. Hmmm, I think to myself, will *nice* be nice enough?

We spend a happy hour making lists of florists to meet, menus to sample, wines to taste and bands to listen to. Eventually the wedding talk winds down and Lily goes home to prepare dinner with her future husband.

I cut up half a grapefruit and mix together a chicken and avocado salad. I make a couple of phone calls and firm up social arrangements for the following week but something is niggling at me, something I should have done. Just as I'm about to sit down to watch an episode of 'Mistresses', I realize what it is. I'd completely forgotten I was meant to go out tonight!

A much-loved friend – Rock Chick Friend, to be precise – invited me to come along to support her son, JB, a singer-songwriter, performing in his first gig. I don't really fancy spending the evening in a noisy pub, but the old Wendy reminds me that Exposure Equals Opportunity. That, together with the fact that I can't let Rock Chick down, sends me rushing into the bedroom where I tear off the granny garb and put on my tightest jeans and some extra slap. Then I totter down the stairs in my highest heels, climb into the car and shoot down Maida Vale to the Good Ship pub in Kilburn.

I have a funny feeling, as I walk through the door into the noisy, crowded venue, that this is not the sort of place to look for my sensible older man. And I'm right. In fact, my FBA (Fit Bloke Alert) goes off about a second later and I feel myself falling off the wagon of my new resolve.

Standing out from the crowd of fans is a friend of JB's, a fine-looking specimen sporting a ponytail. He's looking daggers at three young blondes chatting loudly at the bar. Their raucous voices are drowning out the singer. I drag my eyes away from him and scan the crowd for Rock Chick who waves at me from across the room.

I elbow my way to her side and sit down, clutching her arm excitedly as the first performers finish and her son steps up to begin his set.

Rock Chick and I have a short, intense history. A few years ago, I attended her creative writing course and we became firm friends. Born from hours of late-night conversations about men, dating and the vagaries thereof, we co-authored a book called *Move Over, Mrs. Robinson.*

Rock Chick is Rubenesque, bohemian, seeks a soulmate and likes cats. I'm petite, prejudiced, seek variety and fear felines. We've both enjoyed checkered pasts but are in tune both spiritually and emotionally. This is the catalyst that keeps our friendship flowing.

As JB begins to play I'm conscious of My Little Ponytail (MLP) hovering nearby. By an extreme effort of will, I steel myself just *not to go there.* The draw, however, is stronger than I am and during a particularly romantic riff, I find myself eye-candying him on and off whilst listening to the music. He has an almost perfect profile: large eyes, long lashes, straight nose, good jaw, flawless skin. My fawning admiration catches his attention but I quickly look away. *Come on*, I tell myself. *You promised not to do that any more.*

The noisy girls are still chattering and now I'm glaring at them too. JB's dark, poetic lyrics need to be heard to be understood.

Suddenly My Little Ponytail's eyes catch mine and hold, and I cock my head towards the disturbance and pull a face. He nods in agreement and chemistry along with contact is established. *Oops!* I say to myself. *What just happened there?* But what CBF doesn't see won't hurt her.

When JB finishes to loud applause, I turn to Rock Chick. She's beaming from ear to ear and clapping her hands above her head. We hug each other, so pleased that his debut has been a success. And there, over her shoulder, I see MLP again, heading for the bar. He stops abruptly, hesitates, then turns in my direction, walks back and offers me a drink.

RC looks at me questioningly and mouths, 'Who's *that*?'

'No idea . . . ' I mouth back but the colour rises to my cheeks. I'm a bit flustered by this sudden approach plus I don't want her to think I wasn't concentrating on her son's performance. I climb onto my high horse.

'No thank you!' I answer stiffly as if his very offer was offensive in itself.

'Are you sure?' he insists engagingly, strobing me with the full force of his boyish smile, and before I know it the high horse has bucked me off.

'Why don't I buy *you* one?' I suggest, in an effort to control the situation.

I feel Rock Chick's eyes swivel from me back to him as she waits to see who will score the next point in this 'who-gets-them-in' contest.

'*I'm* offering *you* a drink!' MLP replies assertively which I find masculine and dominant, so I smile sweetly, say, 'Vodka and tonic please,' and off he trots.

Rock Chick looks at me and raises an eyebrow. '*The Girl Can't Help It*, can you, darling?' she smirks. 'It's not your fault, it's in your genes.'

'I'd like to know what's in *his* jeans!' I reply, and subliminally smack myself for thinking such a thought. Although I'm hardly surprised that I can't seem to stay on the wagon for a single evening, I remind myself that this will not – as it may have in the past – lead to rough sex on my living-room floor. It's just a drink, right? *Just A Drink.*

I chat to Rock Chick while he's gone, then her son and the rest of the band come over and join us. They're all on the right side of gorgeous and by the time MLP returns we're pretty much surrounded. I notice his face drop as he hovers nearby holding our glasses, a packet of crisps clamped between his teeth. I motion to him through the throng and pat the empty chair next to me. Looking relieved, he squeezes through and sits down. It's a bit cramped and I feel his leg pressing against mine. Lady Salisbury thinks she ought to move away. Mrs. Robinson disagrees.

We chat about JB's music and how we nearly didn't come tonight. I try to stay on my guard, but I can feel myself warming to him. He's an utter babe and we have lots to talk about but just as I'm beginning to really enjoy the conversation, he mumbles something from which I only make out the word 'girlfriend,' then he gets up and heads back to the bar.

Oh I know I shouldn't be disappointed, but I feel my heart sigh deeply and fold its arms protectively across its chest. I tell myself not to be so stupid; that he and/or his girlfriend have nothing to do with me. Still, I can't help craning my neck to see if I can spot her. There's no sign of anyone who remotely matches him so I decide not let *his* attachment spoil *my* evening and when he returns we continue to chat. I've reneged on the leg deal, however, and moved away to a more appropriate distance. Lady Salisbury is back on the high horse holding tightly to the reins.

The subject of work comes up and he hands me his card. It reads The Plaster Master with his mobile number underneath. The words *you can get me plastered anytime* are on the tip of my tongue but I dismiss them because a) I'm not supposed to be like that any more and b) he's probably heard the joke a thousand times before.

I nod as if impressed and slip the card into my bag. We carry on talking with ease and interest in each other, my flirt-o-meter barely registering above zero.

The fact that I'm a middle-aged writer and antiques dealer and he's a half-Turkish, twenty-something labourer doesn't bother me one iota. Why should it? According to my new principles, I'm hardly likely to invite him home unless my ceiling falls down. It is forward-planning, however, for women on their own to collect tradesmen's phone numbers: you never know when you might need them.

As the evening draws to a close, people start drifting away. There's one girl left talking to a couple of lads at the bar. I ask him outright if she's with him.

'Nah darlin', he shakes his head. 'Me and me girlfriend split up four weeks ago. I thought I told you . . . '

Relief flows through me like hot soup on a cold day. It's not that I like him that much or, heaven forbid, even want him in my life; it's just that he's *really* sweet and *really* good company. That's all.

Rock Chick comes over to say goodbye and I also get up to leave. MLP helps me on with my jacket. As he does so, he whispers in my ear.

'Do ya fancy meetin' up again sometime?'

His breath is sweet; its warmth caresses the back of my neck like a promise.

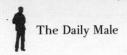

'Go for a drink or somefink?' he adds.

I'm as thrilled as I am surprised. I'm about to say, 'Sure, why not?' when I recall my commitment to Calm Best Friend. I also remind myself of my resolutions, my conversation with Lily, and all the feelings and thoughts that led to my present decision. And so I tell him I'm awfully sorry, but my daughter is about to get married and I'm busy for the next few weeks.

Then, because he looks forlorn and I don't want to seem rude, I retrieve his card from my bag, write my number on the back and return it to him.

Old Wendy says: *Doh! Now you don't have his number.*

New Wendy says: *Good girl! Situation saved.*

He walks me to my car and kisses me affectionately on both cheeks. He makes a move towards my mouth but I push him away.

'Go!' I say firmly, but the feel of his pecs beneath my palms drag me, momentarily, back to the dark side.

'See ya!' he waves cheerfully as I switch on the ignition and rev the engine. I drive home humming a love song, wondering if The Righteous Brothers would like a Sister in their band.

Three

The next day I awake in high spirits, remembering the sweet interlude with My Little Ponytail. I pat myself on the back for having remained more or less resolute and, above all, strong; resisting temptation has never been my forte. A twinge of regret for what might have been comes over me but I do not have his number and that, my dears, is that.

I get up and make my morning coffee, and exercise my way into the day to Gloria Gaynor's 'I Will Survive', the power anthem of every wavering woman.

Once I'm dressed, I call Calm and recount the events of the previous evening. 'And you really didn't arrange to see him again?' she asks, disbelievingly.

'No I Did Not!' I affirm. 'I'm a reformed character, remember? He was drop-dead gorgeous but he's younger than both my daughters' partners and there's no future in it. I am sticking to my resolve. As promised.'

'I'd never have believed it,' she says, like I've just announced my engagement to Methuselah. 'You really mean to go through with this, don't you? Well, I reckon you're going to find happiness with a proper person very soon – make up for the heartache the improper ones have given you!'

'I don't know about heartache,' I say pragmatically, 'but last night's beefcake would certainly have given me indigestion! And one night of passion equals one month of pain.'

I feel very astute for having finally worked this out.

'Well, I'm proud of you,' Calm confirms. 'And how's all the bridey stuff coming along?'

I heave a sigh before I answer. 'We're doing table plans which would be fine if you enjoy juggling unrelated aunts and uncles who have to sit together because there's nowhere else to put them. The best place for them is near the kitchens but you'd be amazed at how much umbrage people take at the geography of their table. There's this family hierarchy. It's a nightmare! I'm looking forward to it but, at the same time, I'll be glad when it's over.'

I put the phone down and devote the rest of the day to my antiques business. My good mood quickly dissipates when I notice, on checking through my bank statements, that what's coming in is disproportionate to what's going out. I either need to curb my spending or up my income so I set off to trawl the antique markets and pick up a few vintage boxes suitable for converting into cigar humidors.

I started doing this in the 1970s. My then fiancé was a keen cigar smoker and I wanted to buy him a special present. The humidors available were all plain, square boxes so I went to Camden Passage, found a beautiful dome-topped, inlaid walnut dressing-case and bartered it down to £24.00. Next, I needed to find someone to convert it into an efficient humidor. Cigars can't be smoked if they're too wet or too dry so the trick is to kid them they're still in Havana where the best cigars have always come from.

The conversion of an empty box into a working humidor involves lining the interior with cedar – the preferred wood in which to store cigars – and fitting it with a humidifier and a hygrometer. The humidifier is a vented unit into which one drizzles distilled water. Humidity is then created when the box is sealed shut because moisture seeps out through the vents and keeps the cigars in tiptop condition. The hygrometer is a clock that indicates the level of humidity – ideally around 70%.

Creating an efficient humidor is an extremely specialized task. Knowing that Dunhill have always been respected in this field, I decided to deploy my inner Mata Hari. I called the Dunhill factory and asked to be put through to the person in charge of humidor production. Most cabinet makers have a little workshop in their garden sheds, so when a man's voice came on the line, I said in a low and secretive tone, 'Don't speak, just listen.'

I told him I had an antique box that needed converting into a humidor, and that if this was something he could do in his spare time, to please write down my number and call me. He phoned that evening and collected the box, which he restored and adapted beautifully.

Men love the allegory that their high-priced stogies have been rolled on the inside of a maiden's thigh, and at upwards of £25 per stick these days, they may feel they're entitled! Rudyard Kipling put it another way when he said, 'A woman is only a woman but a good cigar is a smoke.'

My fiancé was delighted and the next thing I knew, all our friends wanted one. Cigar smoking was hugely popular up until the smoking ban – a pleasure indulged by men and a small coterie of women in a clubby atmosphere or after a meal with fine wines and cognacs. It's gone a bit underground now, but back in the day, it was part of a male-dominated and somewhat elitist culture.

Two years after creating my first antique humidor, I set up a business employing six men all nicked from Dunhill. I supplied many of the world's luxury gift shops as well as many top cigar stores. That kept me busy for the next few years but then times got tough and I had to diversify. I still trawl the antique fairs and auction houses to pick up pieces I have an instinct for; anything that'll fit in the boot of my car, really. I only buy items I love – that way if I get stuck with them, I don't really mind.

If I can turn two or three transactions a week, I'll have some butter on my bread and maybe a little jam too. (Of course if I set up home with an Arnold, I think to myself, I won't have to work at all and I could gorge myself on as much jam as I like. Not that I like jam that much, I prefer peanut butter but that's not the point and I'm getting a bit ahead of myself anyway.)

I spend most of the week working on the business book. I scour the small ads in *Antiques Weekly* for private sales and bargains and try to behave like a grown-up professional without a monkey on my back.

On the Wednesday however, I get an interesting call from Radio Five Live asking me to comment on a piece in the paper entitled 'Women who pay for sex.' Hmmm. I have never *actually* paid for sex, but that's not to say that in the future, if there was nobody around and I really wanted it, I wouldn't consider forking out for the privilege. It's something men have done since time began, and what is natural for one gender ought to be acceptable for the other.

Although I've never handed over hard cash in exchange for sexual favours, I wonder if inviting a young man over for

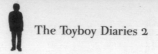

a pre-rumpy pumpy dinner, or putting cinema tickets on my credit card and not getting paid back for them, constitutes *paying for sex*? I don't think so!

If, however, a man I like but do not fancy has taken me out several times without receiving the gift of my body in return, I will invite him out or cook him a meal in order to reciprocate his generosity. That is me paying NOT to have sex but doing the right thing in terms of a respectful exchange.

Four

The weekend arrives and with it an influx of family hell-bent on making the wedding plans as complicated as possible. To prepare for the onslaught, I spend Saturday afternoon diligently polishing the silver and making my signature upside-down pineapple cake. I also bake a batch of Florentines that are so more-ish they may not make it through to tea on Sunday. I like this form of domesticity: I find it grounding. It steadies my mind and the results of my efforts bring their own reward.

With everything sparkling and the preparations under control, I head out for the evening with Blondelicious Best Friend, a feisty girl from whom I draw much inspiration. She may be a Blondie be she's not 'blonde' in the derogatory sense of the word; she's a consummate businesswoman. The three words she uses most often are 'I hate men'. She does nothing of the sort, however. Being long-divorced with three grown-up children, she goes on an awful lot of dates, and some of them, believe me, have been truly awful.

Most recently Blondie has been dating a well-endowed billionaire of seventy. I've followed her through the ups and downs of this particular relationship and am always on hand for counselling and analysis sessions – as she is for me. By listening to her tales and traumas, I've come to the conclusion that for some women, even a billion pounds and a huge cock are simply not enough. Neither are a fleet of classic sports cars and a one-hundred-acre estate.

The problem with Senior Citizen Kane, as Blondie's manfriend has become known, is that he doesn't like London; nor is he interested in cultural pursuits, eating out or shopping. Blondie, being a townie, soon got fed up with hacking up the motorway three times a week to eat Chinese takeaway, swim in the pool and get laid. And months into the relationship, the man – that is to say the Seriously Rich Man – *hadn't bought her a single gift.* 'Why should he?' you may ask – but by the law of supply and demand, if a woman is sleeping with a very rich man, she is entitled to expect a trinket or seven.

Once the initial gloss had worn off – and it didn't take long – Blondie began to pick holes in the relationship. The good part was that his package was apparently massive and more and less worked without hydraulics. The bad part was that everything had to be on his terms.

'Of course it's going to be on his terms,' I tell her as we queue up to buy cinema tickets. 'He's a man – and an old one at that. He's bound to be set in his ways.'

We buy some Pick 'n' Mix to share and settle down to watch the movie. It's not that gripping and my mind soon wanders. Listening to Blondie, I'm pretty sure I don't want to follow in her footsteps despite having promised Calm that I'd give it a go. When we exit the cinema, I run the New Me past her.

'Are you sure that's what you want?' she says, asking me the same question I've been asking myself. 'And can a leopard ever change its spots? Do you think an older man would really make you happy?'

'Only if he's tall, slim, good-looking, minted, well-hung, witty and devoted,' I answer, 'so he either doesn't exist or he's with someone a lot younger than me!'

Blondie laughs. 'Oh ye of little faith!' she says linking her arm through mine. 'Let's discuss this further over a drink,' she suggests, and we head off to the Steele's pub in search of alcohol and adventure.

Sunday dawns and a conglomeration of aunts, uncles and cousins troop up three flights of stairs to my flat. They are here to meet my future son-in-law before the big day.

My mother arrives cashmered, coiffed and manicured, followed by Aunt Bella who looks like she's been covered in Bostik and thrown through the window of an Oxfam shop. Every time she opens her mouth to speak, she shovels her foot in deeper.

'So which synagogue is the service to be held at? And who will be able to give me a lift?'

Lily shoots me a look that says 'Do we *have* to invite *her*?' and I shrug apologetically as I explain the sequence of the day.

'It's a mixed marriage, Aunty,' I say diplomatically, pouring her another cup of tea. 'So we're not having it in a synagogue. The entire function will take place at the hotel. It's very fashionable these days, but if it bothers you, you don't have to attend . . . '.

I can see my mother nodding vehemently from across the table. 'What?!' Bella shouts, her mouth chomping away on a bridge roll slightly out of sync with her teeth. 'And miss the chance of a terrific knees-up?'

My future son-in-law blanches. I know what he's thinking and I stifle a smile. Just the day before, I told him the story of this very same Aunty disgracing herself at Poppy's wedding. Much to everyone's dismay, she took centre stage in front of the band and lifted her skirts to prove that at the age of 78, she could still do the Can-Can. The assembled guests gathered round clapping while Bella high-kicked like a showgirl displaying a pair of voluminous pink satin knickers – which I suppose was better than no knickers at all.

Aunty Billie – as we've always called her – had a very racy reputation. Apparently, during the war she was one of the few women in London parading around in a mink coat and silk stockings when everyone else was shivering in serge and drawing simulated seams up the backs of their legs with eyebrow pencils. How she acquired the glamorous items was anybody's guess, but the words 'on the game' were often whispered. I like Aunty Billie, in small doses. She's a true eccentric and for that, I admire her.

Amid the cacophony of a dozen voices all talking at once, I hear my mobile ring. I'm carrying a laden tray so I let it go to voice mail and more or less forget about it.

'Thanks for coming. Take care!' I call eventually as the last of the elders disappears down the stairs.

'That woman!' My mother protests as she brings some empty cups into the kitchen. 'God only knows what she'll turn up wearing. And just make sure you don't seat her anywhere near me . . .'

Puffing with indignation and in a haze of Jean Patou's *Joy*, she flings her pashmina across her shoulder and limps off out the door. Two broken hips and still going strong.

I hug the future bride and groom and tell them not to worry. Controlled pre-wedding panic is absolutely normal and everything will be alright on the night, sez I. They smile uncertainly and nod, probably wishing they'd eloped to Gretna Green, then they trundle off with their food parcel of leftovers, clutching each other tightly by the hand.

I finish tidying up and flop down on the sofa. What a relief that's done, I think to myself, glad to be able to put my feet up at last. Just then my mobile reminds me there's been a missed call. I pick it up and see a number I don't recognize. Without thinking, I press Dial.

After a couple of rings, a cockney voice answers. 'Ello? ELLO?' it shouts.

It must have misrouted. I hang up but it rings again immediately.

'Wendy?' a man says and I know at once who it is. It's My Little Ponytail! I cut the call in fright then think *Bugger! Why did I do that?*

My heart is thumping and my mouth's gone dry and my stomach's churning like a washing machine. I never expected him to call! What am I supposed to do now?

I dial Calm Best Friend for advice but she's out. How dare she have a life when I need her to advise on mine? I pace the floor and stare at the phone willing it to ring again, but it doesn't. I want it to and yet I don't. My old and new selves have met at dawn and are standing on a windy bluff aiming duelling pistols at one another.

I throw my head back in anguish and let out a frustrated cry . . . and just then, I notice it – a creeping damp patch in the left-hand corner of my living room ceiling.

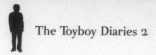

I get up and fetch the ladder. I climb it carefully and reach over to touch the damaged area. The plaster is springy in my hand and a few flakes flutter down to the carpet below. There's a definite leak coming from somewhere. I live on the top floor so it must be a problem with the roof. I climb back down and put the ladder away. Then I return to the sofa and contemplate The Damp Patch thoughtfully.

My mobile is clutched in my clammy hand. I look at it and my thumb flirts with the Dial key. I place the phone down on the coffee table as far away from me as possible and I stare at it, willing it to indicate my next move. It just lays there, all black and silver and silent. Not very helpful at all.

And then, in an Unprecedented Act of Tremendous Willpower To Avoid All Future Temptation, I go into my Call Log and delete the last received number. There. That was brave of me. I'm safe from temptation now.

Five

As the week progresses, I immerse myself in work and wedding plans but I'm frequently interrupted by frantic calls from Lily throwing up matters of global urgency such as: should she have her fringe trimmed this week or next? This provokes a dialogue that takes up way too much time and energy on both our parts.

This is my second experience as Mother of the Bride though Poppy's marriage was a lot less pressurized: I was M.o.B then, but not Hostess. My first husband's second wife assumed that role but she respectfully included me and it was liberating not being too closely involved.

I can see how it's possible for M.o.Bs to corkscrew themselves into the floor with all the organizing they have to do. One woman I know ended up in therapy. Wedding planning should be added to the list of Life's Most Stressful Events along with house moves, divorce and bereavement.

The Damp Patch glowers at me from the corner of the room. The Managing Agents have promised to sort out the roof but I need to organize my own redecoration. I can then claim it back on my household insurance. Hmmm! I absent-mindedly type

'London Plasterers' into Google and scroll down until I reach The Plaster Master.

There is MLP in black and white. What now? Old Wendy knows exactly what she'd like to do, while New Wendy reasons that there are a thousand plasterers in the Naked City so why is she looking at this one? On the other hand, she reasons, a fly-by-night cowboy is always a risk – some cocky so-and-so who'll drink me out of tea and sugar, do a shit job then rip me off just for the hell of it. Logic tells me to select MLP because I've already met him and he's someone I would trust. Both Wendys agree with this, so I make a note of his number and go about my daily work.

At around 6 p.m. my thumb becomes twitchy again. There's my phone, and there's the notepad with MLP's number written on it. I take a deep breath and then I dial him. He answers straight away, the same 'Ello?' I hung up on last week.

'Hi. It's Wendy.' I wait in silence for his response. 'From JB's gig? The other Sunday?'

'Hey!' he answers as the penny drops. 'I called you. You 'ung up on me. Wha'd you do that for?'

'I'm sorry,' I lie. ' I . . . er . . . I had a houseful of people and I couldn't talk. Listen, I've got a bit of a problem with my ceiling. Damp from a leak in the roof. Could you . . . would you . . . be interested in a job? For the ceiling?' I add unnecessarily.

'Sure,' he answers. 'I'll come over and give you a quote. I could make it tonight if you like?' He sounds hopeful.

Tonight? My hair needs washing! My toenail varnish is chipped! And Monday night is yoga night – all of which seem irrelevant compared to seeing MLP again. And, of course, getting the ceiling sorted. Which is the only reason I'm calling him.

'Tonight's fine,' I answer breathlessly and give him my address.

I spend the next couple of hours *not* washing my hair, *not* touching up my toenail varnish and *not* wriggling into my *fuck-me-stupid* underwear. It feels wrong not doing this when a toyboy is coming round, but this is a business matter only, I tell myself, as I pace the floor like an expectant father waiting for the midwife to turn up.

At last the bell rings and I buzz him in. He crosses my threshold, hugs me and immediately admits to being nervous.

'Why?' I ask, wondering if he's going to tell me he's not a plasterer after all.

'Well,' he answers cautiously, 'I wasn't sure I'd see you again – and I've never, er, *been* with an older woman before. I was wonderin' what we'd find to talk about.'

Who wants to talk? appears in a speech bubble above my head.

'I've got a damp patch and you're here to fix it!' is what I actually tell him, but the ambiguity of this statement is not lost on either of us. We give each other a sideways look and burst out laughing. I immediately feel much more like my old self. Flirting is my stock in trade. Keeping Up Appearances is going to be harder than I thought.

Despite these doubts, I handle the visit pretty well. I get out the ladder and point him at the ceiling. He does his Bob the Builder act, sucking his breath in through his teeth and shaking his head. It needs to dry out for at least two weeks once the roof's been repaired, he tells me. Then he'll come back, chip away the damage and re-plaster it.

Come back, will you? I think, as I nod in acceptance and offer him a coffee.

'So how about that drink some time?' he asks lounging casually against the kitchen counter.

'OK,' I say, trying not to salivate at the thought. He is strikingly good-looking but it's the hair that really turns me on. Although it's scraped back into his trademark ponytail, it's sleek and black and shiny. I imagine him pulling the elastic off and shaking out his mane . . . and I can't help imagining what would happen next.

'A drink? Yes. OK. But only as friends,' I add, clinging to the wobbly toyboy wagon.

We book a date for the following Sunday. He kisses me softly as he says goodbye and I feel myself falling like a leaf on the wind.

Wednesday. It's my 62nd birthday and after a lovely lunch with my mother and my daughters, the sisterhood takes me to The Wolseley for dinner. Think 'Sex and the City: The Next Generation' and you'll get the general idea.

Blondie is there looking chic in a cream satin shirt and tight black skirt. She is dodging calls from Senior Citizen Kane and turns her mobile off with a flourish, determined to enjoy the evening without interruption. Sensible Best Friend arrives next. Aged 52, she is happily ensconced with a 61-year-old who ticks all her boxes. She finishes every sentence with 'that's right!' and for her, it is. I envy her for finding a man she relates to on so many levels – not an easy gig at any age. I do wonder though if it mightn't be a tad boring knowing exactly who you'll be sleeping with for the rest of your life.

She's given a lift to Glass-Half-Empty Best Friend, a very attractive yet deeply insecure woman whose cup is never, ever Half Full. A few years ago she was dumped by her husband after almost forty years of marriage. Unsurprising, she simply can't get over it. She's afraid of ending up old and alone and seeks a new man with determined intent.

The internet is her dating playground. However it's fraught with peril because hiding behind their pumped-up profiles lurk lounge lizards, liars and losers. Half Empty has had to learn the hard way that the *well-built Bruce Willis-type with his own transportation company who's willing to relocate* is really a fat, bald, lazy minicab driver looking to put someone else's roof over his own head. She doesn't give up, though, and to give her credit, her stories are only as depressing as her last date. I do admire her and we manage to have a good laugh over some of her more colourful experiences.

'Weren't you seeing someone last week?' I ask, hoping to hear something positive for a change.

'Don't even ask!' she replies and proceeds to regale us with the story of yet another encounter of the disastrous kind.

'I suggested we meet at the Dorchester Bar,' she begins. 'It's not worth leaving home for less, really. And I thought if *he* was no good, there might be someone else there who was.' She pauses to take a sip of her kir royale.

'So I walk in and the only guy sitting on his own is a swarthy, unkempt type in a corduroy cap and a donkey jacket! In the Dorchester! I ask you? I order champagne so my journey shouldn't be completely wasted but I know I'll be home within the hour. He had nothing interesting to say for himself, chewed olives with his mouth open and then used the stick to pick his teeth with – it was disgusting. And when he took his greasy cap off, he looked like he had pubes growing all over his head!'

We all burst out laughing. It's the way she tells 'em. She may be bitter, but she's bittersweet.

The girls and I enjoy our catch-up and later in the evening, Calm Best Friend joins us for coffee. She's also been on a date, but strangely refuses to talk about it. There's obviously potential which needs protecting. Had it been ghastly, she'd have entertained us with the grimmest details.

'Just tell me,' I ask eagerly as she sits down. 'Should I buy a hat?'

She smiles enigmatically. Then, 'Any more thoughts on Dear Old Arnold?' she asks, diverting attention away from herself. The other three turn to me and I'm caught in the spotlight of six impeccably made-up eyes beneath six perfectly plucked raised eyebrows.

'Arnold? Arnold Morris?' Sensible almost shouts. 'That sounds more like it. Are you seeing him? That's right!'

'Not at the moment.' I lower my voice, encouraging her to do the same. 'I'm trying to conform,' I go on, 'but it's hard to give up *boy zone* when I'm not yet into *vest life*!'

They girls laugh raucously. At least they get my puns.

'Your toyboys never last though, do they!' Sensible continues, stating the obvious. 'And then you're on your own again. Arnold on the other hand is . . . '

'Tall, slim and rich, yes, but I can't think of another good thing to say about him!' The girls look at me reproachfully and I relent. 'OK, he's *nice*. He's *lovely*. But the thing is,' I add thoughtfully, with MLP in mind, 'younger men are so much prettier to look at. And I like diversity.'

I ignore CBF who is staring at me pointedly with her lips pursed.

'And, just as importantly,' I go on, warming to my theme, 'they're more interested in women as equals.'

I look across to Blondie who is nodding sagely into her wine glass.

'Older men think because they've got a few quid, they have more human value,' she says. 'They hardly ever ask about you – most spend the evening talking about themselves. And they always fall asleep in the theatre or cinema. Us golden girls are still active and vivacious, but the most exercise *they* get is flipping channels.'

'Arnold is a fit and healthy man,' says Calm, frowning at me.

'Yes, fine, he's *quite* fit but he's – '

'Perfect for you, that's right!' Sensible shrieks. 'And he's certainly looking to settle down. He'll meet someone else if you don't hurry up.'

'I think he already has,' Half Empty contributes, despondently. 'He's gone on a cruise with Elaine Silver.'

'Lucky her. Just imagine it!' I reply. 'Trapped at sea for weeks on end with Arnold Morris repeating the same old stories.' I shudder and close my eyes. 'Seriously, girls, I do want to give up dead-end relationships,' (that is, I *think* I do). 'I just need a little more time to get used to the idea of an older man. Of course, if you could produce a Harrison Ford or a Richard Gere for me, I might consider it.'

'Older men do have their uses,' Blondie cuts in. 'Mine gets his chauffeur to clean my car.' She stops and heaves a great sigh. 'But on the other hand, he farts all night.'

We all wrinkle our well-powdered noses in disgust.

'Well I agree that Arnold could be The One,' Sensible continues. 'You should at least give him a chance, that's right!'

'A chance to do what?' I query. 'Get his mitts around my tits? I think I'd rather play solitaire. Look girls, I know there are pros and cons but I've never slept with an older man before and frankly, I'm terrified. What if his mojo doesn't work? What if I get cold feet halfway through? You have to remember I'm very spoilt in that department. I'm used to long-lasting lovers with fresh, firm flesh, not men with boobs that are bigger than mine.'

'That's a bit harsh!' Calm interjects. 'Viagra deals with the *little problem* but I must confess it doesn't always work . . . ' Her eyes glaze over at some painful memory.

'And when it does,' adds Blondie 'they want to use the damn thing all night! What's worse?'

'There are so many younger single women out there, most men don't want to commit anyway.' Half Empty adds her two-penny worth. 'They've got too many choices nowadays.'

'You'd find more to talk about with an older man, that's right!' Sensible adds.

'It just so happens,' I inform them, 'that younger guys have plenty to talk about. For a start their education is much more recent than ours, and they've all been to Uni which we haven't. Their travel stories are amazing – I went out with one who'd been captured by guerrillas in Guatemala! Or it may have been gorillas . . . '

'Well I still think you're better off with an Arnold than a Tom, Dick or Harry,' adds Sensible, as determined as a terrier.

'Plenty of time for the likes of Arnold when Tom, Dick and Harry decide they want kids!'

Thanks, Blondie. This last comment has the same effect on me as a smack in the mouth, but I laugh it off with, 'They're more than welcome to mine!' and we spill out into the Piccadilly night happy as hell to have each other.

I declined, you may have noticed, from mentioning the impending date with MLP.

Six

Although my date with MLP is only days away, Old Wendy is being insidiously replaced by Even Older Wendy when I find another wrinkle on my face. I ponder booking a firming facial but I'd planned to do this nearer the wedding. In any case, I'm determined not to make too much of an effort this time. MLP has no significance in my life but as I think of his smooth, silky skin, a quiver of desire runs through me. Firming facial or not, will I manage to keep my hands off him on Sunday?

The day before the date, my darling little granddaughters come over to play. One's blonde, the other is dark and they're both quite beautiful. We rehearse 'walking slowly down the aisle behind the bride,' then get the dressing-up box out for them to rummage through. I'm banned from the room as they prepare a fashion show. Tamara parades up and down the corridor in an ancient black evening dress and a pair of wobbly stilettos and Melodie wiggles her little bottom around in a sequined boob-tube and an old Ascot hat. I remember the not-so-distant days when I used to remove their nappies in the afternoon and my lover's Calvin Kleins in the evening, but those days seem long gone now . . . unless . . .

♀

When they leave, I knuckle down to some serious work. Researching the origins of the vibrator for my book on future collectibles, I come across some fascinating facts about the word *hysteria*. Unlike the overused misnomer it has evolved into today, it seems that hysteria was a recognized affliction diagnosed by the ancient Greek philosopher, Hippocrates.

Victorian medics who subscribed to his edicts believed that the condition – literally translated as 'disease of the womb' – was caused by the uterus complaining of neglect. According to Plato, the uterus is an animal within an animal: if it gets out of control, you have to appease it. You go, Plato!

Though not officially acknowledged in so many words, frustrated female Victorians would visit their physicians in a state of high anxiety suffering from what was commonly referred to as 'an attack of the vapours.'

Doctor Feelgood would nod sagely then take it upon himself to grope about beneath the lady's petticoats until he found her vulva. This was thought to be a part of the uterus, anatomical knowledge being a little scant in those days. He would then administer a gentle massage until there was a crisis of the disease, much like the breaking of a fever, and a 'hysterical paroxysm' would ensue. This induced contractions and lubrication and the woman would go away with a smile on her face and a spring in her step.

The condition, however, was not only incurable but also chronic; no sooner had the poor creature got over her malaise than she'd suffer another attack and be back down the surgery for a repeat prescription.

Although the doctors did not consider their intimate ministrations to be in any way sexual (hello?) they did find their efforts time-consuming and laborious. Luckily, in 1869, a team of boffins came up with a steam-powered gizmo they named The Manipulator. Originally designed as a muscle massager, it was found to have extremely satisfactory results in the speedy treatment of hysteria and soon became a must-have accessory for doctors dealing with the disease.

Needless to say, the implement became enormously popular with the *laydeez* who reaped the benefits of the pleasant vibrating action – and in much less time than the hand job! They soon began to request a do-it-yourself-at-home version and the rest is huh . . . huh . . . hah . . . history!

I close the laptop, satisfied with my research, and look at my watch. Only 24 hours to go. I'm looking forward to this date more than makes sense in the circumstances.

Eventually it's 7 p.m. on Sunday and a freshly spruced-up MLP arrives on my doorstep. I swallow hard as he walks in. He's not tall, but he is dark and handsome and my heart can hardly keep pace with my mind. There's a full evening ahead of us. Against my better judgment, he's convinced me to extend the drink to dinner and the cinema. I haven't dared tell anybody. It's not easy living under the shadow of one's own contradictions.

As he pecks me on both cheeks, I find it's me who's nervous. Guilt, trepidation, the breaking of my promise to myself and Calm Best Friend, my goldfish memory, repeating the same mistakes over and over again . . . *What possible future is there with this boy?* I ask myself, as I hang his jacket up. *None. So why do I feel so vibrant?*

I pour us two large Screwdrivers, heavy on the vodka. We clink glasses and chat about our respective weeks. There's a cool confidence about him as he sits down on my sofa, a confidence

I no longer share. What's happened to me lately? I used to be so in control. Now I'm burbling, unable to meet his deep, dark eyes lest I fall into them like pussy down the well. He checks the damp patch – the one that he can see! – which is drying out well since the roof's been fixed, and then we set off out.

He's driving a clean saloon car, which he tells me belongs to his father.

'I couldn't very well take you out in me van, could I?' he jokes. The seductive aroma of 'cock-au-van' assails my nostrils.

'And as me Mum and Dad was stayin' 'ome tonight . . . '

I'm 62 years old and I'm dating a man who lives with his parents.

As we walk to the restaurant he takes my hand, which makes my heart smile. *Now* I know why I'm doing this. He treats me like a lady yet makes me feel like a teenager. The years (as in mine!) just fall away as I bounce along happily beside him, for the night is young and I feel so beautiful. There's a flutter of anticipation between us, a heady buzz of sexual chemistry and mutual attraction. We both know where this might end; we're just not certain when, and therein lies the lure . . .

Despite these oh so seductive feelings, I plan to pursue my resolution. My friends and family may be right, but they can't deny me this: my swansong. MLP will be my 'one for the road'.

We converse easily over dinner then we drive on to the Odeon Marble Arch. He stands behind me in the queue with his arms hugged around my waist and all resolve goes down the tubes as I lean back against him feeling incredibly young, unfeasibly happy and irrationally secure.

He insists on buying the tickets despite my offer to go Dutch. I have an economic dilemma at the box office when I wonder momentarily if I should tell him I qualify for the senior discount. This would reduce his evening's expenditure. I decide, for once, to keep my lip zipped. We haven't done the numbers yet and I'm in no hurry to do so. Most people think I'm at least ten years younger than my age, which is very flattering, and I get quite offended if my Freedom Pass or Senior Railcard are not questioned!

As the night wears on, the schizophrenic thoughts that have been buzzing round my mind for the last few weeks slowly disappear. Old Wendy and New Wendy become less relevant when sitting in the back row of the movies, MLP and I mouth-feeding each other chocolate raisins thereby missing half the film.

When we arrive back outside my home, he double-parks and leaves the engine running.

'Wouldn't you like to come up?' I bleat, mild panic rising in my voice. *Please don't go – I haven't finished with you yet.*

'Course I would!' he replies with a smile, 'I just didn't want to presume nothing, that's all. '

Now I've been out with many a mature bloke who's reversed smartly into a parking space because, having bought me dinner, he's assumed I'm going to be dessert. I find this truly offensive. In any case, even if I did want an older man to climb up to the top floor and make love to me, he could probably do one or the other, but definitely not both.

MLP parks the car and bounds up my stairs like Baryshnikov. He settles himself again on the sofa and I put on a smoochie CD, light the fire and some scented candles and slither down beside him.

And then I discover that he was right: we don't have that much to talk about, because he's kissing me deeply and has slipped his thumb inside my bra and is grazing it gently across my right nipple.

I relinquish all attempts to engage my brain in anything other than the delicious sensations flowing through me. I give his shirt

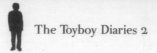

a little tug and he takes it off. Then I allow my skin to dissolve against the heat of his.

He rolls himself on top of me and my desire deepens, all thoughts liquid, morphing to and fro like globules in a lava lamp. CBF's wagging finger loses all significance. If she could feel what I'm feeling now, I know she'd understand.

For the next hour or so, MLP draws me towards the gates of heaven, never quite allowing me to go in. Unable to contain myself any longer, I raise him off the couch and take him to my boudoir where we make unexpectedly slow, sweet love until dawn.

Our first date ends at 5.45 a.m. when he leaves me splashed across my bed, a blissed-out smile on my sleepy face.

The next day is Monday. The phone wakes me at 9.a.m. and without thinking I stretch out a lazy arm and answer it. It's Calm Best Friend. In a sudden panic I gurgle some excuse of having had a terrible night and promise to call her back.

'You OK?' she asks suspiciously.

'Fine,' I say brightly and quickly cut the call. I wonder if I'll have the guts to tell her.

As if on demand, my mobile bleeps. It's a text from MLP.

Hi Hun, thank you for a most romantic and wonderful night. You're a sensual, luvly and beautifull woman. You have my attention at every minute. Can't wait for the next time we meet. Call me if you feel stressed or just need to talk. Xx

Stressed? Why on earth would I feel stressed? Caressed, complimented and cosseted – yes. But stressed? Nah . . . Or at least not until the end of the day when I realize I haven't returned CBF's call. My conscience kicks in and I toy with the phone for a moment, then decide it's probably too late, I should leave it until tomorrow.

Seven

A new old Wendy sails through the week with a smile on her lips and a song in her heart. This is the best part of any relationship: the all-singing, all-dancing delight of wondering what will happen next. All things are possible and promises abound. Maybe that's why I'm addicted to firsts: first nights, first dates, first-time sex . . .

I am, however, slightly anxious as to if or when I'll actually hear from him again. Notwithstanding his lovely text, the night may have been a one off, never to be repeated. And once the swan has sung, is she actually allowed another encore?

To my delight, MLP texts later in the week to say he thinks he left his beanie hat in the cinema. Odeon Lost Property haven't found it, so I offer him a cheeky alternative of where to put his head. I then impulsively ask him if he'd like to come over on Saturday night and cook for me. I get an instant affirmative which sends a thrilling quiver down my spine. I fleetingly wonder what I'll tell CBF about my plans for the weekend. I've been avoiding her calls all week – and she's my best friend!

So excited am I with this future date, I rush out and buy MLP another hat. I hate this look but it gives me pleasure to make the purchase. I can't wait to give it to him on Saturday. And I hope he'll like the beanie too.

Saturday morning. Lily and I set off in high spirits. We have appointments for fittings at Bridal Wear Emporia all over London. I am prepared for the assault on the cliff face of retail: wearing flat shoes, carrying a camera, my handbag filled with bottled water and glucose sweets. This is a military operation; any female will know what an agonizing process finding the perfect dress can be. And a wedding dress at that!

Something begins to dawn on me as we progress through this important day. I'm telling you, girls, this is the biggest scam in history. Bigger even than that Nigerian asking for your bank details so he can pay his millions into your account.

The fact is a White Beaded *Evening* Dress costs X but the very same White Beaded *Wedding* Dress costs the whole bleedin' alphabet. The same applies to *wedding* flowers, *wedding* cake and *wedding* shoes. Don't even ask about bridesmaids' dresses. They put an extra '0' or two on the end of just about everything. My advice is, if you're planning to get hitched: Do Not Use The 'W' Word. You'll be a lot better off.

Lily emerges from the silk-curtained changing rooms looking in turn sultry, silly, over-stuffed and under-whelmed. Several shops later and I'm still waiting for the magic moment when I look up and say, 'Darling! That's the one!'

Some of the assistants are snotty, some are sweet, one treats me with respect, another totally ignores me. I wouldn't buy a gown in her shop if it was the last place on earth.

My mother made my wedding dresses. Both of them. She even made the fabric for the first one. The living room was bedecked for weeks with miles and miles of white satin ribbon, which she cut into strips and wove into a lattice work pattern onto which she sewed thousands of tiny seed pearls. If only I'd kept it, I muse, as I wait for Lily to step out from yet another fitting room.

And then she does, and my breath catches in my throat – for there before me stands my little girl looking like the Grand Duchess Anastasia of all the Russias. My credit card pings at the bottom of my purse.

She smiles at me beseechingly and I gaze back, teary eyed. We both begin to cry, for this is the moment we've been waiting for and this is the dress in which Lily will marry the love of her life and live happily ever after.

After lunch we visit the florist to firm up floral arrangements. Flowers in a circle in the centre of the table? Forget it. Think long-stemmed Calla lilies entwined with crystals standing in metre-high vases surrounded by lilac tea-lights floating in goldfish bowls into which strips of frosted tree bark from the forests of Lapland have been wound. These will be strategically placed on mirrored mats to double the visual effect. The table decorations will look utterly stunning, but from the golf course I hear my ex cry: 'HOW MUCH?!'

As the day takes off its tiara and the teacups give way to champagne flutes, I begin to keep an eye on my watch. MLP is due over around 7 p.m. and Lily's car is parked outside my flat. I must admit, I'm not keen for them to meet. We should be back by 6 p.m. though; plenty of time for me to get ready and for her to head home without them bumping into each other. I can't help feeling on edge about it, nonetheless, especially when at 5.20 p.m., while stuck in traffic, I get a text from him:

Would it be OK for me to ave a shower at urs cos ive finished work early and can come strait over xx

Ah.

Oh.

Er . . .

SHIT!

The last thing I want is Builder Bloke standing on the doorstep when I get back with Lily. I can't text him back and say 'stick to the plan please', much as I'd like to, because a) it would be rude, b) I'm driving and c) Lily is talking nineteen to the dozen about shoes and veils.

Instead I turn my mind to cabbie-mode and whizz in and out the back doubles, tooting my horn and revving impatiently every time a red light looms.

It's all to no avail. As I drive into my road, I see a dusty geezer in paint-splattered combats, a torn t-shirt, plaster-encrusted Timberlands and a sweaty bandana standing at the entrance to my block. Oh mercy!

As I approach, he winks at me and waves. I glower back at him and pull a 'you-don't-know-me' face, flashing my eyes wildly and shaking my head rapidly from side to side. Lily looks at me anxiously. She thinks I'm having a stroke.

Walk away! Ignore us! Go stand outside another building! I shout in my head, hoping he'll pick up my message telepathically.

I loiter in the car but Lily gets out and asks, 'What are you waiting for, Mum?'

I emerge slowly, studying the tarmac with fascination. As we cross the road towards my doorway, MLP smiles broadly and calls 'Orright?' in his thick cockney accent.

Lily stops in her tracks, frowns deeply, narrows her eyes and stares from him to me and back again. It's the kind of expression Her Majesty would wear if she walked in on a topless table-tennis match between a glamour model and The Duke of Edinburgh.

I smile apologetically at Lily and consider saying he's come about my plumbing (which isn't a million miles from the truth). Instead I become flustered, ignore MLP and attempt to rush Lily towards her car. I feel so guilty – we've had a lovely day together and it upsets me for it to end like this, but I am overwhelmed with the awkwardness of the situation.

MLP, bless his youth and innocence, is bigger and better than both of us. He bounds over to where we stand, plants a possessive kiss full on my lips, scrapes his grubby hand down the length of his dusty combats and sticks it out for Lily to shake.

She looks at it like it's a month-old kipper but because she's been well brought up, she shakes it briefly then drops it with a sniff. I notice she doesn't make eye contact with its owner. Instead she shoots me a killer glare and stomps off to her car without saying goodbye. She slams the door, grinds into gear and roars off down the road with nary a backward glance.

My heart plummets down to my boots. I've managed in one fell swoop to upset her, him and myself.

I turn on my heel and go into the block. MLP picks up his bag and follows. I say nothing as we climb the stairs. My mind is whirling: this is the price I pay for down-dating by thirty years and several layers of status. And then I feel even guiltier for actually having thought that.

'I'm really sorry babe . . . that was a bit awkward,' I say once we're inside. 'I wasn't really expecting you two to meet. I didn't mean to offend you but . . . ' I trail off, feeling miserable.

He nods as if he understands but I see the disappointment in his eyes. Disappointment because I did not give him the respect he deserves; disappointment for making it obvious that I was too ashamed and embarrassed to introduce him to my precious little daughter.

In fact, that wasn't at all the case. I'm proud of my gorgeous young toyboys and would like to flaunt them for all the world to see. But I'm also mindful of other people's reactions, especially judgmental children who have no interest in my sex life even if it was *appropriate* – which, to them, it clearly is not.

I send my boy off to have his shower and go into the bedroom. The first thing I need to do now is sort this out with Lily. Judging that she must have arrived home, I call her.

'Yes!?' She answers like a headmistress whose pet pupil has just been caught giving the Cricket XI a mass blow job.

'It's me, darling,' I begin, in a tone of abject apology. 'I'm sorry about . . . '

'Is he old enough to vote?' she demands and I burst into nervous laughter.

'You weren't meant to meet like that . . . in fact, I'm not sure you were meant to meet at all . . . '

'I thought you were on the wagon!' she sniffs. 'You told me you were giving up all that rubbish . . . that . . . that *stuff* you do! You weren't joking, were you? This is the 16-year-old bricklayer you're bringing to the wedding! Oh God, Mum!' she wails despairingly down the phone.

'It's not!' I protest. 'I was joking about that. He really is a lovely guy. We met a few weeks ago – he's a friend of JB's – but it's . . . oh I don't know what it is. Please don't be like this. He makes me very happy . . . '

'I don't need to know any more, Mum,' she says firmly, and slams the phone down.

I sit looking at the receiver for a moment. Every parent will know how soul-destroying the displeasure of one's children can be, whether deserved or not. But then I shrug. Lily is 33 years old now. She doesn't need a Mum in a straightjacket. And as we proved earlier today, we get on extremely well most of the time.

Just then, MLP emerges fresh and fluffy from the bathroom and we begin our sexy little evening. Like Heineken, he reaches the parts other men don't reach, but despite him being charming and pleasing me in so many ways, my mood has been marred: I know that in the eyes of the world, I'm doing something wrong.

Eight

B y the time we've had a couple of Screwdrivers and finished a bottle of wine, I couldn't give a cute cahoot what anyone else thinks. I've shaken off my guilt and gloom, and MLP and I have a heavenly night together. He is both passionate and tender; his body strong and fit, his buttocks tight enough to bounce a ball off. Anyone who doesn't like it clearly isn't getting it.

In the morning, I flip him onto his tummy and give him a sensuous body massage. Then I cover myself with baby oil and slither all over him.

Later, we go for a leisurely walk, buy the Sunday papers and lay around the Elgin wine bar reading them. MLP manages to twiddle his curls, scan the sports pages, drum in time to the music, drink coffee and never break physical contact with me, all at the same time. I love this a lot. He's exhibiting public displays of affection with a woman old enough . . . well let's not even go there.

It's a wrench to see him go at the end of the weekend, and he seems to take his leave reluctantly. We kiss each other, hug at the door and promise to talk the next day. As he trots off down the stairs, I dance along the corridor back to my room. It's time to change those sheets. Massages, especially the oily ones, play havoc with one's bed linen.

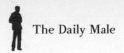

As I go, I catch sight of myself in the mirror. The woman who looks back at me has a sparkle in her eyes and an earthy, satisfied smile creasing up her face. I know her very well.

Wednesday: a momentous evening. MLP takes me to the Emirates Stadium to watch Arsenal fighting – sorry – *playing* Spurs. He confesses to having spent £70 on each ticket and I can't help thinking we could have gone to see *La Traviata* for that (albeit in the crap seats). Obviously I don't tell him this. It's a significant occasion for both of us: he's introducing me into his domain and I am hoping against hope that I'll enjoy myself.

We set off by tube but there are delays and it's obvious we won't make it for the crucial kick-off. At my suggestion, we get out at Paddington and cab it the rest of the way. He sits in the taxi with his head in his hands jigging one knee nervously up and down. I stroke his thigh and rub his back whispering words of consolation – I imagine this is how it would feel if we were on our way to a hospital following a close relative's near-fatal car crash. Thank God it's not. It's only a bloody football match!

Much to his relief, we arrive in the nick of time. Ironically, my Spurs-supporter children are in their caged pen at the same match. I scan the crowd nervously for a minute then relax. I presume – or rather hope – they cannot see me.

I tell him to behave as if I wasn't there so for the next hour and forty minutes he yells, swears, chants, hurls abuse at the referee and the opposing players and picks me up and swings me round every time Arsenal score. It's like being out with a lager lout and I love every minute of it.

♀

I'm still buzzing the following day but have enough tact to tone it down when a girlfriend phones to say she's dumped the man she's been seeing.

I am sympathetic and concerned for her wellbeing but at the same time, I can't help feeling secretly pleased. He wasn't for her anyway, plus her return to the single fold means I'll have someone else to go around with when the famine kicks in. Which it will.

We arrange to meet for dinner the next day and I hang up. After a slight hesitation I call CBF and invite her along too.

Friday dawns with a call from my sister, Marilyn, eager for the low-down on the upcoming nuptials. She lives in Marbella and has done since the Sixties, when she met the man of her dreams whilst holidaying in what was then a small fishing village.

I miss not having her around at this special time. Despite our being very different – saint and sinner come to mind! – we are incredibly close and get together whenever we can. When my girls were growing up, they were very lucky to have an aunty by the seaside and I'd put them both on a plane the minute they broke up from school.

Being four years my senior, Marilyn was meant to look after me as a child, but I guess I was wilful and hard to control. I remember a party we both went to in our teens. We had a curfew of midnight, but when it was time to leave, I categorically refused. She left me there and went off home and I rolled up at 2 a.m. in a car with seven guys. My father was in the street waiting for me. His face, at first wracked with worry, turned purple with apoplexia and I was grounded for three long months. My sister and I laugh about it now but it wasn't funny at the time!

Joined by her brood, she will arrive in good time for the wedding. We're all excited about it; we don't get together nearly often enough.

Later in the day, just when I'm wondering when I'll hear from him again, I receive a text from MLP. I read it, and it brings tears to my eyes.

Need ur body close to mine so I can run my fingers up your spine. Making love until we drop, feel your lips around my cock. Until soon when your all mine, my heart won't stop beating til ur body's next to mine.

It doesn't scan and it barely rhymes and I doubt Robert Browning would have written it to Elizabeth Barrett but to me it's worth the world and then some.

Some women need diamonds, fast cars and five-star holidays to make them feel good. I like those too but not as much as a silly poem written to me by a young man whose sweet sincerity melts my heart.

Later that evening Newly Single Best Friend, Calm and I all meet up for dinner. Calm and I listen attentively to Single's tale of woe about a man she thought herself in love with who simply couldn't love her back. Women are big on investment in men who produce little return. Although she finally recognized this and ended the relationship before he did, it doesn't stop her being really upset.

'I'm getting on for *sixty* now and look at me!' she wails. 'I'm so unhappy. How am I ever going to find another man?'

Calm goes into counselling mode but I tune in to the thoughts swirling round my own head. I hope I never have to base my happiness on 'finding another man'. And this age business! I wish people weren't so hung up on that. I really object to being labeled by my age. For God's sake! It's ONLY A NUMBER! I know 30-year-old fogeys who behave like it's all over and 60-year-old wonder women who are light years away from hearing the fat lady sing. Think young and you'll feel young. And as for getting depressed about being a sexagenarian – why not focus on the 'sex' part?

Calm and I advise her as best we can. We're careful about what we say, though. She and her ex may well get back together before breaking up again for good. I've noticed this pattern time and again, and it can be awkward if you've slagged someone off and then your friend goes back with them.

While this conversation is taking place, a group of four guys have come into the restaurant and sat down at the table next to us. We're in the Union Café in the middle of town, a 'contempary European' establishment with an eclectic cuisine, wooden floors and sparse decor. The ceilings are high and the acoustics fairly deafening. I glance over at them then go back to studying the dessert menu, *all* of which I fancy. That's the desserts. Not the men.

Although ...

When I look up, one of the neighbouring guys is giving me the eye. Oooh! I think excitedly – things are looking up. It never occurs to me that he's staring because I look just like his mother or maybe I have a lump of spinach dangling off my top lip. I sit up a bit straighter and run my fingers through my hair. I offer him a soupçon of a smile and he winks back at me. He's about 35, fair-haired with designer stubble. Not my usual type, but ... Old Wendy is alive and well and pulling in a restaurant in Marylebone.

'So, what have you been up to?' Calm enquires, stealing the moment. Having devoted the evening so far to Newly Single, she has turned her attention to me. I drag myself away from Winky

Neighbour and stammer something about having been to a football match. Damn! Why did I say that?

'And of course, the wedding, the wedding, nothing but the wedding!' I screech loudly, hoping to confuse her.

Out of the corner of my eye, I see Winky frown and turn away. I may have blown that one.

Calm knows me too well to be distracted though, and starts to probe.

'Football!' she cries in mock astonishment. 'Who *on earth* took you to *that*?'

I remain silent and concentrate very hard on a splodge of gravy on the tablecloth. 'I've got a feeling you've reverted to your old ways,' she continues accusingly.

'Whatever gave you that idea?' I ask feigning indignation but I can't fool Calm.

'Well, you've been yawning all night for a start and there's a definite twinkle . . .'

'The guy at the next table just winked at me!' I explain, hoping to put her off the scent again.

She and Newly Single both whirl around to stare at him but Calm turns back and focuses her gaze on me. She's a shrewd judge of character and she knows me pretty well. I know her too and employ more diversionary tactics to distract her.

'Hmmm,' I say seductively, waving the menu in her direction. 'Fancy sharing a Banoffee Pie?'

Calm shakes her head vehemently and straightens her back.

'Not for me, thank you,' she says in clipped tones, willpower emanating from every pore.

'How can you resist?' I go on licking my lips provocatively. 'Cream, banana, toffee, mmmm . . . Surely I can tempt you?'

'No thank you! Not for me,' CBF replies. She's staked her claim to the slimmer's high ground.

Newly Single has retreated into a haze of misery. She is definitely in need of a sugar kick, so I order two pieces of pie and three spoons, just in case Calm changes her mind.

The puddings arrive and for a moment, there's an unaccustomed quiet at our table, except for the moans of ecstasy provoked by the delectable dessert. Calm fights the good fight but loses, picks up a spoon and takes a tiny corner of cake, followed by a larger piece. I shoot a look in Winky's direction but he's no longer interested. His loss. And I've *got* a boyfriend anyway . . .

'That's better,' says Newly Single rubbing her tummy, more satiated than she has been in a year if I heard her rightly. 'So, come on. Football? Spill the beans!'

Since my attempt at changing the subject failed to work for longer than it took to polish off the pie, I decide to embrace my shame and spread MLP out all over the table.

Calm's eyes are quick to criticize. 'I thought you promised.'

'I know,' I moan. 'But it's alright for you. You've both got – or had – sorry darling – someone. I'm not good at being alone. And he's absolutely gorgeous and he sort of . . . well . . . fell into my lap. What was I meant to do?'

'Tip him out again? Just Say No? Walk away?' suggests Newly Single. She gives a big sniff, then nods knowingly. 'Take it from me: if you think it's going to end badly, don't start it in the first place. It's all just a brain fuck.'

'But you never know,' I defend my corner. 'We're having fun and life is short.'

Calm gives a snort of derision. 'So what happened to your new resolve then?'

'If you scrape that plate any harder, you're going to wipe the pattern off!' I say a little spitefully. I want to ask what happened to *her* resolve.

'Remember,' she says thickly, through the last mouthful of cream, 'damage limitation?'

'Yes,' chips in Newly Single. 'And look at your past experiences.'

'It'll end in tears,' sighs CBF. 'You know it will.'

'Oh give it a rest,' I mumble turning away from their well-meaning but twisted mouths.

I hate these conversations. I fear the girls are right. I drive home feeling rattled, confused and a little depressed.

Lying in bed that night, I try to concentrate on the book I'm reading but my brain keeps whirring instead. Knowing it's a self-fulfulling prophesy, I now want to rush through this relationship and come out the other side. I'm tired and emotional and I need to pay more attention to my own edict: *by all means have your legs in the air, but for God's sake, keep your feet on the ground.*

I fiddle around on my mobile composing a self-preservational text:

If I was halfway sensible I would end it now before I get hurt. I like you a little too much for my own good. Sorry, but I know exactly where this is headed . . . but I don't send it.

I think about the facts instead. I'm a post-menopausal grandmother who thinks she's still 18. From past conversations, I know MLP wants to get married and have children, and so he should. He obviously can't do this with me – there's the minor matter of a 33-year age gap to consider! – though funnily enough, that was totally irrelevant when we were in the bath lapping champagne from each other's clavicles, or sharing chocolate-covered

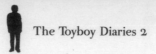

strawberries while working through the Kama Sutra with Ravel's *Bolero* blaring on the iPod.

I really need to get this into perspective, I think as I drift off to sleep. It's just a bit of fun, and when it's over, I promise to revert to my original plan.

Nine

I wake up with a jump, my hands clamped across my ears. I'd been dreaming that all my friends and relatives had ganged up on me and were shouting 'Stop! Stop!' at the tops of their voices into my face.

I shake myself fully awake and jump into the shower, alternating the hot water with the cold to blow the dream away. I feel jittery and out of sorts. I can't concentrate on ten minutes of yoga and I certainly don't feel like working today. I decide to have a pedicure instead. A little pampering will do me good. And tonight, since I do not appear to be seeing MLP – or anyone else for that matter – I shall treat myself to a 'Me Date'. I'll buy all sorts of goodies I never normally eat and slob out on the sofa in an old tracksuit with an avocado and mango mudpack on and I'll watch four episodes of 'Grey's Anatomy' back to back. And then I might lick my own face.

I go for my pedicure, but despite the soothing foot massage and strains of whale music playing in the background, my mind refuses to relax. By my calculation, I haven't heard from MLP for six whole days. The calendar marches relentlessly towards Valentine's Day and there isn't a date in sight.

♀

For the rest of the week I submerge myself in work, but by Friday I can't stand it any longer. I've been given two complimentary tickets for a comedy club, a perfect excuse to text MLP and invite him out. After waiting three hours for the favour of a reply I finally receive one: *very tyard but not bothered as long as we're relaxing im not sure that I'll be v. responsive tonight anyway.*

His acceptance of my invitation pleases me; the tone of it does not. Is this what I need? A 28-year-old fossil-in-training? I bin the comedy idea and go out and spend a week's income on a fat, juicy steak instead. I figure I can always slap him round the face with it if he's late then use it afterwards on the black eye.

I don't know why I'm suddenly feeling so aggressive towards MLP. He's never *not* turned up; he's always caring and sweet with me. It's not his fault if he's *tyard* . . . although his inarticulacy is starting to grate. It compounds the differences between us. I'm usually so fussy about things like that. How did this one slip past the Spelling Police?

As I prepare the meal for him, I wonder whether the talk with Calm and Newly Single is behind this. Perhaps it had more of an effect on me than I care to admit. Their condemnation of my social choices is subliminally chipping away at me, doing a great job of eroding my confidence. I don't trust my own judgment any more – or is it that I'm simply facing up to truths I've known all along?

I shake my head to purge the negative thoughts and give the steak an almighty thwack with the tenderizer. There! That feels better. Maybe I should get a part-time job in an abattoir – somewhere I can channel my aggression on defenceless lumps of meat. I'm probably just angry with myself for having got involved with

MLP in the first place. It's not his fault – it's mine: anything he's ever done to upset me has taken place inside my own head. He is a good, decent, caring, genuine, polite, helpful honest human being . . . but if he's not calling or texting every hour, on the hour, I turn into the Wicked Witch of West London.

MLP arrives that evening more or less on time and my heart melts when I see his darling face. He looks so lovely: clean and scrubbed, hair neatly slicked back and smartly dressed. He's ready to go straight out, but looks mighty relieved when I tell him we're staying home instead.

I cook the dinner and he eats with gusto, then he does the washing up and we go through to the living room and out onto the balcony. It's a balmy night and he stands behind me and wraps his arms around my waist. I lean back and angle my buttocks towards him and am overjoyed to feel him grow hard against me.

Desire rises swiftly and he moves my hair aside and nuzzles my neck. My breath quickens as I feel his erection straining the cloth of his jeans. I reach back to stroke him. He undoes his fly, then brings his hand forward and unzips mine. The street below is quiet and we giggle at our naughtiness as we lower each other's trousers. My panties quickly follow. The Man in the Moon blinks indulgently then averts his gaze for the sake of our privacy.

MLP thrusts into me from behind and I stand on tiptoe to receive him. We writhe in rhythm, enjoying the risky business of possibly being caught *in flagrante* by the neighbours. I hold the wrought-iron rail tightly, nervous that he might get over-excited and topple me off the balcony. The position we're in is not very comfortable but MLP continues to slam in and out of me and climaxes suddenly, withdraws, puts himself away and steps back inside.

I'm left high and dry halfway to paradise with my trousers round my ankles. My hormones are all over the place. I grit my teeth and suddenly decide we need A Talk. Looking back, what I actually needed was An Orgasm.

I tidy myself up and go back inside. MLP is spread out on the sofa, smug and self-satisfied, eyes drooping on the verge of sleep. I stand over him, arms crossed, and plunge straight in.

'How would you feel if tonight were the last night we spent together?'

He bolts up onto one elbow and looks at me as if he's about to burst into tears.

'It's not,' I reassure him, 'but how would you feel if it was?'

'I'd miss you!' he objects. 'A helluva lot! I'm very attached to you, I think about you all the time. I talk about you all the time. I just wish . . . I wish . . . I wish I was older!'

I shake my head. He reaches for me, and I sit down and take his hand. I whimper at the sweet innocence of the man. He could so easily have said he wished that I was younger.

'I love being with you, Wend,' he says simply. 'When I come round here it's like coming home. And the way you look after me, cook for me – you make me feel like a very special man.'

'You are a very special man,' I say. 'I'm sorry, I don't know what came over me,' *or didn't come,* I think. Then, in a moment of inspirational circumspection, I suggest the following: -

'Shall we continue to enjoy the basic fundamentals of life which are food and sex? Because really, what more do we need from each other?'

He hugs me tightly and nods enthusiastically.

'And one day, when the time is right,' I go on, assuming the role of compassionate elder, 'you can phone me up and say, "Wendy, I've got a son".'

He blinks. So do I. My maturity and largesse astound me. So do my mood swings, because I hardly want to play Fairy Godmother to some ex-toyboy's kid by another relationship.

Tonight there is such sweet sorrow to our being together. We feel very strongly about each other yet we both know a future is impossible. I really love him and in his own way, he loves me; yet I can hear the clock that chimes 'Goodbye' ticking, and the sound is growing louder.

MLP stretches languidly and tells me that his back and legs are aching. I spread a towel out in front of the fire and motion for him to lie there. He undresses down to his boxers and I sit astride his beautiful body and give him a long, slow, sensual massage. I could baby-oil his skin forever; it's so smooth and soft and I feel so at one with him in the fire's glow.

I roll off his back onto the floor beside him, and we begin to make love again, gently at first, then as intensely and passionately as we ever have. I snatch at the sands of borrowed time as they slip through my fingers and though he's here and in my arms, I sorely feel my looming loss.

We lay together naked, caressing and telling stories till late into the night. He says he loves listening to the way I talk, that he tries to express himself better when he's with me, to use a wider vocabulary and articulate more. I stroke his hair and kiss his mouth; the mouth that will one day say: 'I'm sorry, I can't do this any more.'

I reach for his discarded t-shirt and pull it over my head, then I get up and go into the kitchen to put the kettle on.

'I have one more question,' I say over my shoulder as I hear him come in behind me.

'Is it a serious one?' he asks, sounding slight anxious.

'Yes,' I reply. 'Very serious indeed. I need to know, each time we say goodbye, when will be the next time we say hello.'

He looks relieved that it's not *that* serious.

'Maybe Valentine's Day?' he says tentatively, and reaches for his cup of tea.

The next day's a work day. MLP leaves early and I roam around the flat picking things up and putting them down. I'm the one who's *tyard* today – I never sleep well with a man in my bed. I tidy up the kitchen and later, glancing at the mantelpiece, I notice an invitation to a cocktail party at the Bolivian Embassy that I'd completely forgotten about. I've neglected my social life recently what with organizing the wedding and seeing MLP whenever he is available. I finger the elaborate, cream-coloured card, run a manicured nail over the embossed wording. A party might be just what I need.

At 5 p.m. I go to my wardrobe and slide the hangers across until I find the dress I'm looking for. Black lace over flesh-coloured satin. Perfect. I wash and dry my hair, redo my face, pull on some sheer tights and high-heeled satin shoes and check my reflection in the mirror. *You'll do,* I say out loud to the foxy lady looking back at me and I sashay out the door.

As I park my car in Eaton Square, I notice a good-looking man standing in the street with a glass of wine in one hand and a half-smoked cigarette in the other. I enquire if I'm at the right address and he starts chatting me up. As I make to leave, he hands me his business card boasting an unpronounceable Hungarian name with a title in front of it. I reciprocate with mine (card, that is, not title) and enter the grand, stucco, Belgravia building in search of my hosts. I network a little, make acquaintances out of strangers, swipe canapés off passing trays and neck a couple of glasses of Bolivian Chardonnay.

Every now and then, Baron Czykzyncsky von Lech appears through the throng, undressing me with his eyes and subliminally slamming me up against the wall without buying me dinner first. He's not my type but the interest restores my confidence.

My friends and I go to Mimmo's afterwards, where I'm introduced to the elderly but amusing Sir John O'Groats who invites me to be his squeeze at the Berkeley Square Ball. I accept graciously, happy not to have to fork out the £150 for my own ticket. However, squeeze he won't – not this peach, at any rate.

It's been a fun evening and I tumble into bed and stretch out like a starfish somewhat more contented than before.

Valentine's Night. The butterflies carry me through the day and at 8 p.m. MLP arrives on my doorstep in an immaculately pressed shirt which he fills to perfection. His muscular thighs are straining at the denim of his jeans and I can hardly wait to rip them off him.

His handsome face is hidden behind a bouquet of the most exquisite crimson roses wrapped up in cellophane and tied with an enormous bow. He places the arrangement on my kitchen table and stands there grinning. Then from behind his back, he hands me a heart-shaped box of chocolates and I hand him an ice-cold bottle of champagne. He pours us two kir royales as I have taught him to do and we toast the occasion. My cup runneth over all down my chin. I send him to the sofa while I finish in the kitchen.

When everything is ready, I call him in for his first taste of caviar. He bites into the cracker a little uncertainly then rushes over to the sink and gobs the whole lot out like Tom Hanks in *Big*, scraping the world's most expensive snack off his tongue like I've fed him some evil poison. He accompanies this puerile act with a medley of gagging noises. I'd have found this pathetic coming from anyone else, but from him it's sweet and funny and utterly endearing.

I screw the jar back up and return it to the fridge, quickly rethinking the first course. I throw together a warm goat's cheese salad then follow it with my special recipe chicken soup, because he's had a chest infection and I want to make him better.

The next course is *Boeuf Stroganoff* with green beans. I round off the meal with raspberry jelly, prepared in a heart-shaped mould, which I manage to turn out neatly onto a plate without it flopping all over the floor. We spoon this into each other's mouths with copious amounts of extra-thick double cream.

My idyllic evening of love and romance is only marred by the fact that Arsenal is playing Bolton in the FA Cup Fourth Round. This important match obviously has to be watched out of the corner of one eye whilst attempting to give me his (less than) full attention with the other. We repair to the living room as Bolton equalizes in the 90th minute. An extra half hour of play? I can hardly contain my joy. I resign myself to the fact that as we've been 'going out' for over a month now, this is the sort of thing I will just have to put up with. After all, boys will be boys.

I imagine he'll make it up to me once the game is over but his lovemaking tonight is a little light on altruism and a little heavy on self-satisfaction. I snuggle up close hoping to get him

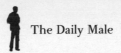

re-started, but he's already fallen asleep. I lie awake for a while, listening to the raindrops pattering on the trees outside my window, soothed by the sounds of the wintry London night. I sniff his skin, inhaling the musky scent of him and pucker up my lips against his chest. As I fall asleep, a small voice inside my head replays the well-meant warnings: *damage limitation*, it says softly . . . *it'll all end in tears . . .*

Halfway through the night, marvelling at the fact that MLP isn't snoring for once, I stretch out a leg to make contact with him. All I find is an expanse of cold, empty bed. I listen for his breathing and pat the mattress anxiously – he's gone! I wriggle across to check the floor in case he's fallen out, then I leap out of bed, peep into my en suite and set off in mild panic to search the flat. I find him asleep on the couch wrapped in a bath towel. His breathing is laboured due to his bad chest and I can only presume he left because he hadn't wanted to disturb me.

I tiptoe back to bed feeling guilty, wondering if I should cover him up with a spare duvet. The heating's off and it'll get cold towards dawn, but I fall back to sleep before putting this act of mercy into practice.

The atmosphere in the morning is a bit strained, but we get over it. MLP has no work today and nothing to go home for. He wants to hang out with me, it seems. I have a couple of business appointments and am obliged, therefore, to take him along. This feels like being a working mum with a child on half-term holidays, though he does the driving which helps a bit.

We run across Knightsbridge hand in hand to see the buyer in the Cigar Department at Harrods. He confesses to it being his first time in the store and then snogs me voraciously on the escalator. I am half tickled pink, half mortified (the parts of me that are pink you cannot see). I've been a supplier of humidors and vintage crocodile-skin cigar cases to Harrods for many years now, and being seen *in flagrante escalatante* by the staff may not do a lot for my reputation. I really should have sent MLP home this morning, I think to myself. But then again, when he's with me, I feel he's mine. When he's not I fret and pine.

We arrive home in the pouring rain and race inside. MLP unties his hair and shakes it out like a wet dog. Taking my cue from Mae West, I suggest we *slip out of these wet clothes and into a dry Martini*. He exits the bathroom wearing The Robe (long story . . . for which you'll need to read my other book, *The Toyboy Diaries I*). I change out of my grown-up gear into my lilac Juicy Couture tracksuit. Then I make us tea and crumpets and we snuggle up together on the sofa.

My phone rings, bursting the bubble I've created around us. 'Go away!' I shout at it, but a moment later, it rings again. Mindful that it might be a child in need, I lean over and glance at the screen. Two missed calls: Lily and Calm. Two of the dearest people in my life, neither of whom will understand why I don't want to be disturbed at this particular moment.

I sigh deeply, extricate myself from MLP's embrace and call Lily back.

'You'll never guess what I'm wearing!' she says jovially.

'What?' I ask hurriedly trying to speed her up.

'I'm walking round the flat in a pair of thick sports socks and my wedding shoes – so as to stretch them out a bit!'

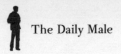

'Good idea, darling!' I compliment her. 'Nothing worse than shoes that pinch and a bride with an agonized expression on her face! Anything else you need me for? I'm a bit . . . '

She wants to chat about other stuff, but for now, I don't. I rush the conversation along, tell her I'm sorry I have to go, blow her a kiss and hang up. Guilt brews up inside me like froth on a pint of Guinness.

MLP is lying on his side watching television. I spoon back into him and he suckles my earlobe, letting me know by the thrust of his hips exactly what he'd like to do next. I wiggle my ass in assent and he tugs my trousers down and enters me from behind in full view of *Richard & Judy*. I assume they won't mind. Viewers behaving badly are better than no viewers at all.

Although I relax sufficiently to enjoy his lovemaking, the tension will not leave me completely. I know I shouldn't have rushed Lily off the phone and if she knew the reason why, she'd absolutely kill me. This all feels wrong and self-indulgent, having sex on a 'school day' afternoon. I should have sent him home this morning; God knows, I have enough to do.

Jen

The next week is filled up with family, friends and a race against time to get some work completed before The Big Day. Despite my full agenda, though, MLP is never far from my thoughts. The strains of 'Mad about the Boy' accompany me wherever I go.

I'm just about to text an invitation to secure his company for the weekend when I realize, with a sinking feeling, that it's me who's making all the running. The words *it'll end in tears* buzz round my head like wasps at a picnic. I try in vain to swat them away.

My heart soars later when a message comes through from him. He has some Big Exciting News: it seems he has a very good chance of getting tickets to the Millennium Stadium to watch the Arsenal-Chelsea Coca Cola Cup Final next Saturday! It takes me a millisecond to process this information. Then I realize what it means:

He's going to be away next Saturday in Cardiff!

THAT'S FUCKING CARDIFF NEXT FUCKING SATURDAY!!

I know I'm being a hypocrite – that it's absolutely fine for me to have plans but TOTALLY OUTRAGEOUS if he does – but I just can't help myself.

I put down the phone in a black depression then break all the rules by texting him again. *Your message has left me sad. Have we lost something? We've had such a lovely time so far and I want that to continue but I need your reassurance that you want it too.*

After about an hour he replies: *Nothings gone anywhre. Just need some space so things can run more smoothly. I'll be down as soon as I can get away.* Like he lives in the bloody Hebrides.

The only words I can see in this text are 'need some space'. Don't people say that when they want to finish with you?

When Lily calls later to ask if she can come round to talk table plans, I quietly sigh. When Poppy wants me to babysit Tamara and Melodie, I inwardly groan. I manage, however, to paste a smile on my face when they all turn up, relieved to lose my blues in Mummy-mode. We sit down for tea and the little ones, as always, take my mind off my self-inflicted troubles. *This* is the real stuff of life, I think later as I tidy up their toys. So why am I wasting my time on one particular plaything when it comes without a safety certificate and is likely to fall apart in my hands?

Come Saturday, I'm feeling more positive and putting MLP as far out of my mind as possible, I go over to Newly Single to play Scrabble.

As I'm on my way home at 11.30 p.m. the phone goes off. It's a text from him: *We won! Goodnight babe. Have a good sleep xx*

Like a hug to my heart, I feel inordinately grateful.

The next week, on Wednesday, I go to pick up Tamara from ballet. While waiting for her to emerge from the changing room I re-read all MLP's saved texts. I wish I had the recipe to preserve that early time. Why does it dissipate so quickly?

One of the other mothers starts talking to me and I flip my phone shut guiltily. I really should concentrate on one thing at a time. Being with my grandchildren is very precious to me, but my love life lives like a beast in my brain, squirming and restless, keeping me on edge.

'How was the dancing, darling?' I ask, as I take Tamara's hand and lead her to my car.

'It was boring!' she answers. '*Point and stretch and point and stretch!* I'd like to learn tango next term. Ballet's really quite babyish.'

I smile at her words and put my arm around her. She cuddles up to me then I drive us to her favourite café for tea. While she tears lumps off an apricot Danish, she tells me about two different boys she likes at school.

'You've plenty of time for all that!' I warn. I look at her innocent little face and dread the traumas she's got in store.

'That's what Mummy said,' she answers. 'But she only goes out with Daddy. You go out with lots of men, don't you, Didi?'

I can't help but laugh. It's not what'd you expect to hear from a nine-year-old and at the moment, I wouldn't wish my lifestyle on anybody. 'Yes, I do,' I admit. 'But I'm very naughty!'

Tamara looks at me steadily for a second or two. Then she grins, wrinkles up her nose and says confidingly, 'You know something, Didi? I like being naughty too!'

I love being with this child-woman. She's very astute yet has so much of life to learn. My most fervent hope for her future is that Cupid should be kind to her.

♀

On Thursday I wake up feeling restless and unsure again. MLP's Valentine roses are drooping on the kitchen table, their bloom fading, their petals dry, their stalks no longer standing straight and tall. That's not unlike the way I'm feeling. I wrap them up in newspaper and throw them in the bin. Maybe I should consider doing the same with him.

On Friday I rise early and set off on a day trip to Edinburgh to research hotels for the Fringe Festival. This is a highlight in my social calendar, a jaunt I organize annually with a group of friends. Much as I try, I cannot ignore the fact that I haven't seen MLP for two weeks. I know this shouldn't matter, but unfortunately, it does.

Stuck in traffic on the drive to Luton, I'm amazed and delighted to receive a spontaneous text from him:

Have a good day in Edinbruh. Let me know when ur bak. I miss u x I can't believe he remembered! I don't need a plane now! I'm flying without wings!

Will do babe, I text back. *What are you up to?* which is my way of screaming: WHEN AM I GOING TO SEE YOU?

I spend the rest of the day awaiting his reply. Finally, as I'm driving back from Luton, I receive it: *What time was you planning to get home? X*

I bite the bullet and dial his number. All this texting is doin' me 'ead in.

'Hey babe!' he says warmly when he hears my voice. 'I've just come out the shower. Gonna get dressed now.'

I mistakenly assume he's on his way over to see me. Instead of confirming this, however, he tells me that he's hurt his foot playing football and is therefore going out to play snooker *with the lads*.

'FINE!' I bark, then slam my phone shut and fling it over my shoulder, a move I immediately regret. What if he rings back?

Spinning along the dual carriageway just off the M1, I unhook my seatbelt and turn around to grope frantically on the floor and the back seat. When my eyes return to the road, I have drifted across the central reservation and am about to be totalled by a dirty great truck hurtling down the hill towards me.

MLP may be worth something, but he's certainly not worth this. With my heart thumping at this horrifyingly near-miss, I slow my speed to 20 miles an hour and drive the rest of the way gripping the wheel like some grey-haired granny who's finally passed her driving test after 35 attempts. I arrive home in a right state, light a cigarette and march into my bedroom.

What on earth am I doing? I no longer smoke and not only am I smoking now, I'm smoking in my bedroom!

I march back into the kitchen, douse the cigarette under the tap and try to get a grip. I call Blondie but she's out. I leave her a message that I'm free for films on Saturday. I need to have some-thing arranged as I'm clearly not seeing my so-called *boyfriend* any more. Luckily for him. Should he walk in now I'd probably plunge my fist down his throat and drag his bollocks up through his oesophagus.

Mindful of the fact that I haven't eaten and might therefore have to add starvation to my list of sufferings, I stick a potato in the oven. This is one of the potatoes I bought for him. I never buy them for myself: fattening, carb-ridden, pasty white things,

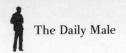

potatoes are. I love chips though. And mustard mash, and crispy spuds roasted in goose fat . . .

The potato sits there, squat and solitary in the middle of my oven with the broken light which he's promised to fix for me several times but hasn't.

O melancholy potato, borne of the womb of blessed Mother Earth, why are we both so lonely?

I'm talking to vegetables now.

Thanks, MLP.

I groan and reach for another cigarette.

At 7 p.m. on Saturday evening I'm out with Blondie for a pre-cinema bite to eat. She takes one look at me, dismisses the menus and orders us two large vodka and tonics.

'How *are* you?' she says, gazing intently into my face.

No point whatsoever in saying 'Fine!' so I launch into a mammoth moan about life in general and toyboys in particular.

'Oh darling,' she says, full of sympathy. 'Didn't you once tell me that "a man should be an accessory in your life not your entire wardrobe"?'

'Probably,' I answer dejectedly. 'But what I say and what I do currently have no connection with each other.'

She orders another round of drinks. 'Why would you think that this one was going to work out better than any of the others?'

'I don't know,' I reply. 'He's just . . . lovely. And he seemed so keen at the beginning . . . '

'They always do,' she sighs. 'He knows as well as you do there's no future in it. Once the sex begins to pall, there's not a great deal to look forward to.'

'Except more sex?' I suggest.

Blondie shrugs. 'They can get that anywhere.' She's nothing if not realistic.

'Look sweetie,' she goes on with compassion, 'you have to ride the lows, because you so enjoy the highs. But never forget you have a choice. You could have any man you want . . . '

'No I couldn't!' I argue, and list all the men I've wanted who haven't wanted me: Warren Beatty (c.1975), Robert Redford in 'The Way We Were', Johnny Depp in anything and Patrick Dempsey (preferably in *me*). I'm rambling now but she listens attentively. As we leave for the cinema she gives me a hug and suggests I ought to nip this in the bud.

'Not you too!' I say despairingly. 'I thought you of all people would be supportive.'

'I am,' she argues, 'I just can't bear to see you like this.'

We buy our Pick 'n Mix and settle in our seats. I leave my mobile on just in case, concealed between my legs beneath my coat. I'm not expecting anyone to ring but I live in hope.

At a particularly crucial moment in the film, the phone begins to vibrate. I jump out of my skin and grope around my crotch in a most unseemly manner. Excitement reaches fever pitch when I see a text from MLP but swiftly plummets when I read it:

Hope your not cross with me hun. Will speak tomorrow xxx

Cross?!

Cross!!??

I slam the lid shut and stuff it back under my coat disturbing all the people around me. I'm now in a terrific huff. Don't let anyone tell you that age and experience bring dignity. Thankfully Blondie is asleep and therefore oblivious to my erratic behaviour. When I calm down, I realize that I've completely lost the plot: of the film and, more seriously, of my own life.

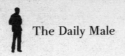

Twenty minutes later, my phone vibrates again. The same demented grappling takes place.

Please alow me make it up to you? I'll start tomorrow morning with a supris. C u then x

Omigod! Tomorrow's Sunday and he's going to turn up on my doorstep to find me looking like an unmade bed. Plus I have a ton of stuff to do before the wedding, *and* I need waxing. Notwithstanding this, I'm beyond delighted so I hug my arms around myself and nestle down in my seat to dream the rest of the film away.

Eleven

Sunday morning. My alarm goes off at 7.03 a.m. and I follow my instinct into the shower. I spend thirty minutes doing my make-up to look like I'm not wearing any, then waft around the flat with the lightness of a meringue. At 8.30 a.m. I get a text from him: *Hi babe I've broken a bone in my foot. What do you want for breakfast?*

I wonder if these two sentences are in any way related. I also wonder how he plans to get up my stairs.

At half past nine my doorbell rings and what happens next is the most thoughtful and romantic thing anyone has ever done for me.

My boy limps in carrying a bouquet of yellow roses, a box of Godiva chocolates and a carrier bag from the immorally overpriced local deli containing: two cappuccinos, four fresh croissants, a loaf of nutty, seed bread, half a pound of rich Cornish butter, six organic eggs, a jar of homemade raspberry jam and a piece of wonderfully oozy Brie. I feel as though the expression 'blown away' was coined especially for me. How could I not adore him?

After breakfast, we turn day into night and go to bed where we make blissful, kiss-full love till noon. We get up slowly and go to Lots Road Auction Rooms where I have some antiques business to attend to. I enjoy having him hobbling along beside me and introduce him to a couple of Louche Lovejoys, who only raise their eyebrows imperceptibly.

In the afternoon, I leave him snoring on the sofa while I go to visit my children and my mother for the minimum possible time. I cancel my evening arrangements which were supper and Scrabble with a couple of married friends. I would not have let a single friend down . . . but on the other hand, I might.

We go to *Ping Pong* in Westbourne Grove for dinner. Densely happy from the day's events, I speed-neck two very strong Mojitos then do the stupidest thing a woman can do whether under the influence or not. When he gets up to go to the Gents, I text him: *I luv u x.*

The minute I've sent it I want to disappear into a ditch and die. I am so embarrassed by the impetuous action of my drunken thumb that I pray he's left his phone at home so I can delete the message before he opens it. He returns to the table and carries on eating and I begin to relax, thinking my prayers may have been answered. Halfway through the next course however, his back pocket suddenly goes off. He brings his phone out and reads the text while I find myself studying the contents of my duck spring roll with all the fascination of an archaeologist who's just discovered Atlantis at the bottom of his garden pond.

He reads the message, says, 'Aaah', smiles at me, pops the phone back into his pocket and carries on eating. I start gabbling to fill the space, my voice too loud and much too fast, as I attempt to erase the happenings of the past ten minutes. I dig and dig, wishing someone would take the spade away and smash me over the head with it so I could fall into the hole and shut the fuck up. How dare the Mojitos do my texting for me?

He sets off home after dinner, and I'm back to wondering if/ when I'll see him again.

I'm woken early on Monday morning by a call from Calm Best Friend. She tells me she bumped into Arnold last night at a Charity Ball.

'He looked divine in black tie,' she tells me encouragingly. 'He really is in great shape. He asked after you actually.'

'You sound like you're trying to sell me an antique carpet! And you told him I was waiting for him with open arms, I presume?'

I hear the triumph in her voice as she answers. 'Stand by your phone! There'll be a call very soon.'

I suppress a groan. 'But I don't *want* to . . . ' I whinge, sounding remarkably like I used to when my mother told me to eat my greens.

'Yes you do!' she chirrups. 'You have got to give Arnold the benefit of the doubt. One date? One evening out of your so-called *busy* life? How bad can it be? He'll take you somewhere fabulous and you'll have a super time. Do it for me? Please?'

'Alright,' I answer grudgingly. 'I haven't had a treat for a while,' unless you count MLP's breakfast, but I can't talk about that.

'Good girl!' she says exultantly like I've done all my home-work and got an A+. 'You won't be sorry!'

I'm not so sure.

A few days later, MLP calls to ask if I want to get together again. I'm still mortified about the *I luv u* text but I am, of course, over-joyed to hear from him. We make an arrangement and it's not

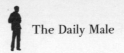

until after I hang up and replay the conversation in my head that I realize he sounded a little troubled.

The night arrives and so does he, a little late as usual. After a dinner of fresh asparagus Hollandaise, followed by a rack of lamb and roast vegetables, we settle on the sofa and have a few drinks. I begin to relax.

I'm sucking the individual fingers of his left hand when I suddenly decide I've had enough of him wearing the ring his previous girlfriend bought him. He professes not to be able to get off, so I go into the kitchen for some olive oil, which I smother over the offending digit. Eventually, after much twisting and turning on my part and crying and yelping on his, I manage to extricate the silver band from him. I now feel he's more mine than before and I tell him so. He smiles uncertainly.

Because I'm annoying and I can't leave him alone, I then proceed to re-open the closed-up piercing in his right earlobe with a rather girlie diamond ear stud. I read somewhere that possession is nine tenths of the law. I seem to be determined to put this into practice.

It's after midnight when I take a candle from the table and he follows me to bed. We lie face to face in the flickering light and gaze into each other's eyes.

He is preoccupied and a sinking feeling grips my heart as he says, 'I need to tell you something.'

The *tears* it's going to *end in* prickle the backs of my eyes.

'Is it bad?' I whisper, my voice quivering like the candle.

'Prob'ly not, but you've got to listen . . . ' He laughs nervously and too loudly for the mood in the room.

'You know when you texted me . . . '

Oh God. 'I waspissedIdidntmeanit – '

' . . . And you said you lu – '

'It doesn't count!' I say frantically. 'I didn't spell it properly. And I really regretted it afterwards – '

'But you said it to me one other time,' he interrupts.

'No I didn't! Did I? When? I don't remember . . . '

'You did. In the car once. Anyway, listen. Just be quiet and listen. I like everything about you. I like being with you. All the time. There's not a moment in the day I don't think about you. I even Google Earthed your flat the other night to feel close to where you live. But . . . ' he pauses, searching for the right phrase. 'LOVE . . . to me . . . it's such a *big* word. And people misuse it. It's, like . . . ' he checks through his vocabulary, '*enormous* . . . and I would never say it unless I really, really meant it. I just wouldn't.'

'I know,' I interrupt, simply to stop him talking. 'It's OK baby, I quite understand. It's just that when I'm with you, I get overwhelmed sometimes and . . . and . . . '

I want to say 'and I can't help myself because I really do love you,' but after his little speech, I know I can't.

MLP is soon asleep, snoring quietly. I lie awake, staring up at the moon, which is staring down at me. I know I've been a fool, allowing myself to fall so heavily for this boy. And this conversation has really brought it home. I stay awake for quite some time, thinking of all the advice my friends and loved ones have given me, struggling with how topsy-turvy my emotions have been since MLP entered my life. As my eyelids droop and I finally fall asleep, the midnight demons come to call, filling my dreams with their mocking laughter as they point their crooked fingers at me and berate me for a fool.

♀

The next morning I wake MLP with a kiss and a cup of tea. I'm just about to climb back in beside him when the phone rings, ruining my artful plan. I'm tempted to ignore it, but smile apologetically and mumble, 'I better get that, just in case . . . '

I hurry to the living room to grab the receiver. It's Arnold! After a hurried 'Hello, dear, how are you?' he invites me to the opera followed by dinner at The Ivy the following week.

A refusal is on the tip of my tongue but then I stop myself. Why not? I promised Calm I'd give Dear Old Arnold a chance and I need to stick to this.

As I'm finalizing the arrangements, I hear MLP pad into the kitchen in search of breakfast. I hang up, feeling furtive, then go and wrap myself around him.

'Who was that?' he asks.

'A friend,' I say casually. 'He's . . . er . . . got a spare ticket for something.'

I then tell him I have paperwork to do and after breakfast I ease him out the door. He asks a few questions about Arnold before he goes and I think he may be jealous. Good. He's been talking about going to Turkey for three months to build himself a house.

'When you're away this summer,' I ask him jokingly as we hug goodbye, 'am I allowed to go out?'

'Absolutely not!' he replies. 'You have to stay home at all times and wait for my calls.'

Sad thing is, the way I feel now I probably would.

Twelve

I have a good productive week forging ahead with my book on future collectibles. Thank the Lord and Tim Berners-Lee for the internet! So much information in such a small space, it really is a time- and life-saver.

I enjoy the cyber journeys into unknown territories – wandering through the old French quarter of Shanghai or studying the soaring value of cast-iron moneyboxes made after the American Civil War; it keeps my mind occupied. Immersed in work, I hardly think of you-know-who at all. Well not *all* the time, anyway.

I spend a couple of evenings at home. I sit in front of the TV juggling place names and table plans and fielding increasingly panicked calls from Lily about The Big Day. I'm in the middle of a particularly steamy episode of 'Holby City' one evening when the phone rings. Irritated at having to miss a crucial part of the plot, I answer snappily then soften when I hear my daughter's voice.

'Mu-um?' she asks with the whine I've come to know and love so well (not!)

'I've got this odd couple who don't know anyone and I've no idea where to seat them. I met her when I was away travelling, and he's a friend of a friend who now isn't coming. Funnily enough, they're both gay, but I don't suppose that means they'll end up together! Could they go with the Spanish cousins, do you think?'

I heave a sigh. The Spanish cousins will be talking Castilian.

'Isn't there anywhere else you can put them?' I ask. 'Why can't they go with your young friends?'

'Because we've got two tables of ten already and these two odd extras . . .'

'I'll tell you what,' I interrupt, an idea having come to me. 'I'll call the hotel in the morning and see if we can increase one of the tables for ten to seat twelve. They might be a bit squashed, but hey! OK? Can I go now please? Connie Beecham is just about to have it off with the dastardly new doctor and I don't want to miss it!'

When I get into bed that night, I remember that last time MLP was here, we didn't make love. In fact, that was the case on our last two dates. The trouble with sex is that it generates the desire for more sex, except when you're married or with a long-term partner, of course. I get to thinking that it really ought to be pre-scribed on the NHS as part of a health and fitness regime. Doctors should recommend five orgasms a week to be taken before, after or during your banana, beetroot and blueberry smoothie.

As sex is deemed to be so good for you and becomes harder to obtain in later life, it ought to be made available to the over-sixties in the same way as bus passes and free prescriptions are. I may start a campaign.

In its instinct-driven, loveless, reproductive form, it's something rather basic. However in its emotional, tender and romantic state, it can become addictive; not so much for the act itself, but for the feelings of wellbeing it engenders. A lot of post-menopausal women have zero libido but because I'm on HRT mine is as potent as it ever was. You can, of course, go into hibernation when no one's around who interests you, but you can also come roaring back to life as soon as that chemistry bell starts to ring.

Sex with someone you like (as opposed to the tramp who sleeps near the cash machine and keeps making lewd remarks at you) generates a spiritually uplifting effect on your chemical levels and these produce a free remedy for a whole range of mental and physical problems. Just prior to orgasm – here comes the science! – the brain emits a dose of oxytocin, a sedative which mimics morphine in a natural way. The production of oestrogen, which rises when a woman is physically involved, can help ease a multitude of ills and is an effective painkiller. (On the other hand, if the person you're having sex with is a pain and you want to kill them, write to me privately and I'll give you some tips.)

It's also documented that when you are sexually aroused, your pulse rate increases from 70 to 150 beats a minute: that's much the same as a weightlifter's. One good session burns off the same amount of calories as running on a treadmill for 15 minutes, so if you do it every day and desist from stuffing your face with cake at the same time (not a particularly seductive look in any case), you could lose half a kilo in a week. Is there any comparable diet on the market? I don't believe so.

Having sex on a regular basis also protects against viral diseases as the blood becomes saturated with antibodies and that's why the Pope always has a runny nose. Don't argue. Next time you see him, check it out.

And the best news for all of us is that frequent intercourse enlarges women's breast size temporarily by up to 25%. You can even raise your IQ by having an orgasm, as during that crucial moment, your circulation speeds up to its maximum potential. This would be the optimum time to apply for membership to Mensa, though how you would co-ordinate the two is something I have yet to work out.

As Thomas Szasz, the Hungarian psychiatrist and academic put it: 'In the 19th century, masturbation was a disease. Now it's a cure.'

Perceptive chap, old Tommy, I think, as I close my laptop and head for bed.

At 8 p.m. the following Tuesday, on a lovely spring evening, Arnold picks me up and takes me to the opera. I sit sleepily in the dark womb of the theatre playing with the strands of hair caught in the elastic band I removed from MLP's ponytail, which I now wear around my wrist. It's hardly Cartier, but to me it's more. During a particularly moving aria, Arnold attempts to hold my hand. I remove it from his grasp to clap when the tenor has finished singing, and then tuck both hands neatly between my crossed legs. The message reads: No Entry Under Pain of Death.

Arnold is, however, elegance, eloquence and charm personified. I can see what my friends are talking about. On paper, this really is the kind of man I should be with: he complements me in age, culture and experience and although at 69 he's not exactly 'Love's Young Dream', I have to admit that neither am I.

We have a pleasant dinner afterwards discussing a multitude of subjects, and while he's paying the bill, I try to imagine myself doing it with him. At the moment of congress, a firewall crashes down in my brain saving me from taking the thought any further. He holds my arm protectively as we leave the restaurant to cross Upper St. Martin's Lane and I acknowledge that this feels considerate and protective but nothing more.

He parks outside my flat and switches the engine off. I stiffen slightly and a flicker of alarm sparks up as he turns to me expectantly. I feel an obligation to invite him up for coffee. Once inside, I put all the lights on and some rather upbeat music. No crackling log fire, no scented candles. I know what message I'm sending out, but I doubt he does. And I'm right. Because suddenly, in the middle of a conversation, he takes my chin firmly in his hand and lunges forward to kiss me. I'm quite taken aback but go with the flow so at least I can say I tried. I wonder if I could film us unobtrusively through the camera in my mobile and forward it to my friends for their approval?

The kiss isn't bad. What riles me though is his assumption that he is entitled to it without any provocation whatsoever from me, the kissee. Then, without encouragement or invitation, Arnold suddenly pulls off his cashmere polo neck and reclines on my sofa. I am as shocked as a nun who's just been goosed by a Cardinal. Maybe more shocked.

With growing trepidation as all the lights are on, I dare myself to look down at his body. He's not bad for his age, but as hairy as a bear.

'Oooh!' I say, trying not to make it sound like 'Eeuwh!'

My young men tend to be smooth-skinned and sinewy. They take great pride in their appearance, using grooming products and moisturizers. They shave themselves: sometimes chests, but always, *always* down below. This obviates the need, after oral sex, to go to the dentist for a haircut. Neither do I need to vacuum the bed sheets nor remove the dreaded curlies from my bar of scented soap.

I do not intend to find out what forests lurk below Arnold's waist tonight. I clear my throat then stand up and start fussing with a floral arrangement on the table. I attempt a lightweight laugh that comes out sounding like a hyena being tickled by a porcupine.

'Get dressed, Arnold, you'll catch a cold!' I say in my most matronly manner.

He takes this as some kind of clarion call, grabs my arm and tries to pull me down on top of him. With a rictus smile pasted on my face so as not to offend him, I deploy my own military to resist the army of his advances.

'Not tonight, Napoleon,' I say. 'I've er . . . '

Got a headache? Got my period?

'Er . . . ' I struggle for words even as I struggle from his amorous clinch, 'I've had a really lovely evening, thank you,' I pant (not in a good way), 'but you've just come out of a relationship, and I think it best for now if we remain as friends.'

Phew! That didn't sound so bad, did it?

He rather grumpily sits up and pulls his polo neck back on, expels a puff of wind as he struggles slightly getting off the sofa, thanks me for the coffee and slinks off down the stairs.

First thing the next morning an excited CBF calls to enquire about the previous night's date.

'Well?' she asks.

I sigh.

'*Well?*'

I choose my words carefully. 'There's no doubt he's a very, very, very nice man . . . ' I say, then grind to a halt.

'But?' she says after a silence.

'Oh sweetie, but everything! I don't fancy him. I find him a bit pompous. He repeats himself with the regularity of a grandfather clock.'

'Did you even give him a *chance*?' asks Calm crossly.

'I did!' I squeal. If she could only see what I endured. 'I *did* invite him up and I *did* let him kiss me. I just couldn't go any further. I'm sorry . . . I just couldn't. Arnold, bless his woolly old socks, is *not* the man for me!'

'He could grow on you?' she suggests.

'He could grow runner beans in his chest hair for all I care, but I'm not going to eat them!'

Calm is quiet a moment, seemingly digesting this comment. Then she bursts out laughing. And that effectively ends the Arnold debate.

It occurs to me later that Dear Old Arnold, aka DOA, also stands for Dead on Arrival, which, in the circumstances was rather appropriate!

Friday. I haven't heard from MLP for a week. I suppose I could get in touch with him but something is holding me back.

I go to my cupboard and sniff the shirt he left behind like the answer lurks somewhere beneath the armpit. I consider cutting off a sleeve and sending it to him like some sinister Cosa Nostra message: *Next time it'll be your arm.*

I decide that if there's no message by 6 p.m., I'll call him.

The deadline comes and goes. I extend it to 7, 8, 9 and then 10 p.m.

Eventually, not being able to bear it a moment longer, I prepare a text:

Hiya! Hope you're OK. Do we have a problem? x

It takes me half an hour to compose these nine words, and me a writer . . .

But I don't send it. Instead I go to my wardrobe for yet another sniff then I check to see if my Lucky Ladybird is still patrolling the bedroom window. She is not. I eventually find her dry and lifeless on the bathroom floor, as dead as a dodo and as stiff as my next drink.

I retire early to seek oblivion, my mobile clutched like a life line in my hot little hand.

Thirteen

Saturday. The message comes through early and wakes me with a start.

Hey babe. Wat u up to tomoro?

Nothing! Nothing! And even if I were, I'd cancel it! I want to shout. Having been a victim of ITS (Impetuous Thumb Syndrome) for way too long, I resist replying until I have reflected on my options. Tomorrow is Sunday. Although I have a family do in the morning, the afternoon stretches before me like a life sentence for a crime I didn't commit. I want to see MLP – but, really? Is it wise? I'm at a crossroads now where I have the alternative of hurtling down Heartbreak Highway until I crash or pulling in at the next services to take a break. It occurs to me, however, that I'd rather swallow another slice of heartache than have to eat at a Little Chef.

The fact that MLP has contacted me spontaneously forces my foot down on the accelerator and, ignoring my short-lived misgivings, I invite him over for a late Sunday lunch. Then I throw on some clothes and set off to sail happily up and down the aisles of the good ship Waitrose, enjoying my food-shopping foreplay.

♀

At 10.30 a.m. the next morning I arrive at the home of my first husband and his second wife to celebrate the circumcision of their first joint grandson by the son of both their second marriages to each other. Are you keeping up?

I have a rather complicated extended family. A lot of the people who married in the Sixties subsequently divorced and married again. Some gave birth to new families, which provoked a plethora of half-siblings, steps and exes all of whom are here today. These include:

The hosts.

Their joint son and daughter-in-law with the new baby.

My elder daughter's half-brother who is my first husband's second wife's son by her first marriage.

My son-in-law's mother and stepfather.

My son-in law's father and his children by his second marriage to a woman who isn't there because he no longer talks to her.

My younger daughter from my second marriage and her fiancé.

The dog that my second husband's ex-partner left behind which our joint daughter is babysitting because her father's playing golf.

And a lot of small children making a lot of big noise.

I'm friendly with all these people because I've actually managed to work out who they all are, and the children get on famously, even though they're not entirely sure to whom they belong. This is my life; these are my people. Moses may have asked Pharaoh to *Let My People Go*, but this morning I need them to stay.

I've never attended a circumcision before and I'm pleased to note it has all the elements of a cutting-edge *cock*tail party.

Circumcision is one of the oldest known surgical procedures in medicine, dating back some 15,000 years. For Jews and Muslims, the ritual is a mandatory part of their religion, but African, Aboriginal and Aztec males also choose to chop, the reason being that those who traditionally inhabit hot, dry climates do not wish the sand to get into their nooks and crannies thereby causing irritation.

Interestingly, in Madagascar, circumcision is practiced in 100% of cases regardless of religion. The procedure is dictated by the women, who maintain that circumcised sex is 'longer, stronger and cleaner'. Those Madaboutit girls sure know their own minds.

My granddaughter, Tamara, step-cousin to the baby in question, is morbidly fascinated by all things gory and wriggles her way through the crowd till she's standing mere feet away from the action. I follow closely behind. If a penis, no matter how small, is about to be displayed, I'm right there in the front row.

It also happens to be Purim. This is one of our more joyous Jewish festivals, celebrating yet another deliverance from oppression, when we traditionally don fancy masks and costumes, drink too much syrupy wine, eat indigestible food and spend the night in the bathroom.

In the spirit of the occasion, the *mohel* (surgical rabbi) is dressed in a sober, dark suit topped off by a cheap nylon Tina Turner wig. This is slightly surreal and some of the other guests mutter that it's unhygienic and inappropriate. I find it hilarious.

The baby boy lies on his grandfather's lap, his little legs spread-eagled like a spatch-cocked chicken. The parents hover nervously nearby, the mother sobbing quietly into a scrunched-up tissue. The *mohel* takes the baby and holds him aloft reciting a prayer of

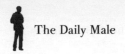

benediction, then swabs his innocent bits liberally with iodine, pulls the excess skin up through a sort of cigar cutter, reaches for the scalpel and with one swift *swish!* whips off the overspill.

The baby bawls momentarily and bleeds like a stuck pig (definitely not kosher). However his wails are drowned out by cries of *Mazeltov!* and everyone begins to clap and sing. Glancing around, I notice the women all look like they're sucking lemons and the men are clutching themselves in horror at the received memory.

Tamara is nonplussed by the whole experience and wanders off to play Solitaire on her mother's Blackberry. What a child of the Noughties she is! I go in search of smoked salmon and herrings and pass the rabbi's worktable on my way. Lying there abandoned, already drying and shrivelled, is the little piece of foreskin. It reminds me of the story of the *mohel* who collected so many he had enough to make a wallet. It was, of course, a magic wallet for when he rubbed it, it turned into a suitcase. That's one for the Chanukah wish-list.

The event passes the morning and at 1 p.m., just as I'm about to leave, my children invite themselves back to mine for lunch. There is no Jewish mother on God's green earth who doesn't enjoy feeding her flock, but today of all days! What can I tell them? I have a fridge full of food for someone I shouldn't be with and a whole horde of hungry offspring dying to be fed. Remorse at refusing them threatens to overwhelm me. I should, of course, text him not to bother, but do I? Do I, buffalo. Instead, I blush crimson, apologize profusely, mumble something about a prior arrangement and watch them slink off, disgruntled, towards the nearest Pizza Express. Although I feel awful, I console myself: they have each other while I . . . well, I have . . . I have . . . what do I have exactly, other than a social life with more twists than Chubby Checker?

I rush home to prepare the food. Then I change my clothes several times, eventually settling on a black lace pants and bra set with stockings and suspenders, a black denim skirt with a zip-up front, a black and white low-cut top and black suede, high-heel boots. It makes me feel sexy but stupid. This is a casual Sunday lunch we're talking about here, not Dominatrix Day at Madame Cynthia's.

He's due at around 1.30. The chicken, potatoes and parsnips are roasting in the oven, the rest of the food is sitting expectantly on the worktop drumming its fingers and looking at its watch.

At 2 p.m. I'm bouncing off the fucking walls.

I rubberneck out the window, a little flutter of excitement running through me every time a car turns into my road, but none of them stop. Finally one does and reverses into a parking space. It's a great big Audi so is obviously not him but I still flatten myself against the cold pane to get a better look. A well-dressed blonde gets out. I suppose it could be him, but only if he's dyed his hair and had a sex change.

I contemplate the waste of money, buying all this food, and make a contingency plan to eat the chicken for the rest of the week, dump the potatoes in the bin and make a soup with the vegetables. The guilt *vis à vis* the children returns to taunt me like a finger-wagging ghost.

At 2.15 p.m. I walk up to the hall mirror and slap myself hard a couple of times round the face. That feels better. I should have done it earlier.

Just as I'm about to reach for a Stanley knife, MLP arrives with some of the Sunday papers I've already bought. I'm so happy to see him, I wouldn't have cared if he'd brought me last season's Arsenal programmes. I throw my arms around his neck. He kisses me awkwardly then stands back to look at me. I enjoy the appreciation in his eyes at the trouble I've gone to in both my appearance and the delicious meal – which, as always, he thoroughly enjoys.

I send him to the sofa while I finish tidying up the kitchen. When I'm done I find him leafing through the *Sunday Mirror*. He throws it aside and pats the cushion next to him.

At that moment, my mobile rings. It's Dear Old Arnold again! I thought I'd got rid of him! I kill the call but take a second to readjust my face. MLP looks at me questioningly.

'It's . . . er . . . just an old friend.' I explain. 'No one important.'

I throw my phone dismissively onto the coffee table, confirming my total disregard of this 'old friend', which seems to ignite MLP's ardour. He grabs me possessively by the arm and pulls me down astride him. He kisses me deeply and raises his hips and I grind down onto his burgeoning erection. He slides his hands up my thighs and discovers the stockings and suspenders, which stoke his rising fire.

For the next couple of hours we make abandoned, wine-soaked love on the sofa, the floor and then in bed. Finally, we lie spent and sated in each other's arms.

And then I let him sleep for he's fulfilled his obligations, which were:

1. To turn up for lunch.
2. To make love to me.

Not that difficult a remit, surely?

He awakes in the early evening and wanders dreamily into the kitchen, wearing The Robe, with his mobile in his hand. I'm doing something interesting with the leftovers – stuffed peppers – and I turn around and smile at him, oblivious to the fact that my life is about to hurtle headlong off a cliff.

He's standing there reading a text he's just received, twirling a curl and frowning. A presentiment of doom swirls malevolently around my head like a pea-soup fog in a Fifties thriller.

We sit down to eat supper. He's abnormally quiet. This doesn't worry me unduly until he suddenly says:

'Er . . . Wendy . . . ' and I drop my cutlery with a resounding crash and instinctively put my hands across my ears.

'I don't wanna hear this!' I say, because I know – I just KNOW – what's coming. He never calls me Wendy. 'Hun', 'babe', 'oi! you!' yes; but never Wendy.

'You have to,' he says calmly. And I do. And the pain of a thousand poisoned arrows shoots through me, leaching its venom into every crevice of my viscera. What a terrific appetite suppressant that is!

I don't know if there was any particular moment when MLP began to go off me and based on the antics of the afternoon, it's not a question I care to ask. Was it something I'd said? Something I'd done? Some over-demand I'd made? The need in my eyes last time he left my bed? The way I look in the mornings without my make-up . . . who knows? All I know is that now this long-expected conversation is finally happening, I'm totally unprepared for it.

'A girl arxed me out last week,' he says matter-of-factly.

'And did you go?' I question calmly.

'Nah . . . it wouldn't've been right.'

We sit in silence as I wait for him to continue. He's eating all the while, chomping away on the meal I so lovingly prepared for him. Between mouthfuls he explains that he met a girl down the pub. They got on well, and she confided to his friend that she really liked him. His considerate friend has just texted him to impart this thrilling news. I sit in silence trying to rewind the day by an hour or so.

'I'd . . . ' he pauses, swallows loudly, 'I'd like to go out wiv 'er but I wouldn't do that while I'm still seein' you. I'm not like that.'

I look at him and shrug. I don't really trust myself to talk, but as the capable, cope-able, older person at this 'party', I know that talk I must.

'I went out with another guy last week but it meant nothing to me. And I always said I would never hold you back.'

The one I call *My Sad Tape* is playing on the retro kitchen cassette. Gerard Kenny croons 'You Are My Fantasy' and Barry Manilow tops it off with 'Somewhere down the Road'. It could be my choice of music that eventually drives them away. Maybe I should invest in the Hardcore Bastards or the Pus-Filled Maggots, but why should I buy music that I don't like only to get stuck with it when they walk away?

I suddenly feel unable to continue this conversation any longer so I scrape my chair back from the table, throw my napkin onto my still full plate, and stomp out onto the balcony, snatching up his cigarettes and lighter as I go. I light a fag and draw deeply on it, resulting in a terrific head rush. On top of a hastily necked vodka and the shock at what he's just told me, I'm now feeling giddy and slightly sick. I look down onto the street below and imagine myself falling, my scream piercing the night like his words just pierced my heart.

Is he worth that? Definitely not. My children and grandchildren don't deserve it either – not for a long-haired, oft-unemployed Essex boy who, incidentally, always refused to go down on me.

I stay outside shivering, more from fear than cold, waiting for him to come and find me, and eventually he does, drawing me gently back inside.

'So who was this guy you went out wiv?' he asks, batting my hostility back at me.

'No one,' I answer. 'Just a guy. An older man.'

'Better than me?' he asks.

'At what?' I snap. 'Quantum physics? Oral sex? I wouldn't know.'

'Do you want me to go?' he asks. *NO!* I scream inside. It's hard enough dealing with this while he's still here – if he leaves, I'll fall apart completely. I push past him and go into the kitchen for a glass of water. His trainers are lined up neatly against the skirting board and I pick them up and hide them in the broom cupboard. That's bound to stop him leaving, isn't it? *Lost me trainers? Oh I'd better stay wiv 'er forever then.* The pathetic futility of this gesture is my tipping point and the deepest sadness sweeps over me.

I return to the living room and slide onto the floor at his feet. I crouch between his knees and take both his hands in mine. I look up at him and try to speak, but my voice keeps cracking like bad plasterwork – something he'd know nothing about.

'I just want to thank you for everything,' I croak, as a big, fat tear rolls down my cheek and plops onto his combats. 'Thank you for all the lovely dates. Thank you for Valentine's night, and that lovely breakfast you brought round. Thank you for always turning up when you said you would – more or less. Thank you for all the sexy texts – at the beginning anyway . . . '

I trail off. I don't want him to see the impact he's had on me, nor make him feel guilty because what has happened is really not

his fault. And I especially don't want him to see how he's actually made me feel: which is very, very old.

I get up and we sit like strangers on the couch though he's certainly more relaxed than I am. And why shouldn't he be? He's been fucked, fed and fussed over and he's offloaded me in a reasonably decent fashion. And now he has a new girlfriend to look forward to – life must seem pretty terrific!

After a while, I get up and walk back out to the kitchen. He follows me, looking around for his trainers. With a sense of absurdity, I open the broom cupboard and hand them to him. He looks at me like I'm peculiar or something, then goes back into the living room to put them on. I remember his t-shirt and get it from under my pillow. I hand it to him without meeting his eyes.

We stand opposite each other in the hallway and I take his face in both my hands. I turn it left and kiss that cheek, then turn it right and kiss the other one, the way a mother would kiss a cherished child who's leaving to pursue their life.

'Talk to you later!' he says cheerily.

I raise one eyebrow.

'Or tomorrow or the next day,' he goes on.

I open the front door and out he walks.

I set my mouth in a thin, straight line and I march into the bathroom. I pluck The Robe off the back of the door and stuff it into the washing machine. That way it'll be nice and clean for its next wearer whoever that may be.

Things never end happily do they?

They just end.

Fourteen

I open my tearful eyes and squint at the bedside clock: 05.28. Dawn on Monday. The memories of last night come creeping back, scraping away at my karma like cat's claws on an old chair leg. I have a dragging sensation of something terribly wrong in my life. I gather the duvet around me feeling lost and alone. I close my eyes again to seek the sanctuary of sleep, but sleep don't come easy when your mind is in a mess.

The selfish sun shows no sympathy and beams me out of bed and into the coldest shower I can bear. How dare it shine when I'm so miserable? I turn the radio on. Laura Brannigan is singing 'Gloria'. I mouth the words but choke up when I get to the line *if everybody wants you, why isn't anybody calling*?

I pick up my weights to get some endorphins pumping and fight off the melancholy, but my heart feels as heavy as a rock in my chest. It'll take more than exercise to get me through this, I think.

Lunchtime comes and goes but the fridge remains unopened. Some people comfort-eat away their sadness; I seem to want to starve mine to death. I go out onto the balcony and stare down at the park. MLP made love to me out here not so long ago. And now I've been dumped. How did that happen? And why so fast?

I watch the locals ambling to and fro: children, dogs, joggers, a small group practicing tai chi. Amazing, really, how life goes on even when your world is falling apart . . .

At teatime, I pull myself together sufficiently to email my publisher to tell him that the business book is taking shape. I ask if he wants to suggest topics for additional chapters – 'I'm raring to go,' I type, though a less raring person you couldn't hope to meet. Like that old music hall song 'My Word, You Do Look Queer', perhaps if I tell people I'm fine, then maybe I will be.

At 5 p.m. I decide it's time to venture out, to get a little air. I go to check my face in the mirror and shudder at what I see. If this is what the latest break-up has done for my looks, I need to change my strategy or harden my heart, and fast! I slather on some moisturizer and attempt to put some make-up on, but the tears keep rolling down my face, moistening my mascara which streaks through my foundation creating a salty, smeary paste. Madame Lauder would not be impressed.

I put on dark glasses and head out to the shops to see if I can animate my appetite for dinner. Although a flat stomach may be one benefit of this break up, a three-day migraine, which is already brewing, definitely is not.

I take deep, re-energizing breaths as I walk quickly down the road. When I get home, a little refreshed, I prepare a stir-fry then settle down on the sofa to make a few calls.

I spend the evening telling anyone who'll listen about the very sorry story of the end of the affair. This is the road to hell: every time I tell it, I tell it better, and the better I tell it, the more upset I get. The Sisterhood are suitably sympathetic, but remind me that I must have known it was finite and isn't it better that it ended now before I had time to get attached? Hello!

♀

Over the next few days, I discipline myself to only think about MLP for three minutes in every hour. He is absolutely forbidden to live rent-free in my head. I don't want to love him and I don't want to hate him. I just don't want to care.

I invite the girls over for a catch-up. I make a Caesar's salad and a giant lasagna and although I vowed I wouldn't mention it, I bewail the fact that, apart from the wedding, I've got nothing to look forward to, no romance on the horizon. Sensible suggests I take up Bridge. I know it's a brilliant game that many people enjoy but I never planned to learn it until I was old. The thought that this could be *now* fills me with dread. I flash forward to a group of biddies sitting round a table, their gnarled hands shaking slightly as they struggle to hold the cards. I notice that one of them is me so I push the Delete button. Hard.

The sisters also suggest I go online: 'Times Encounters', 'Independent Heartbeats', 'Help Me! I'm a Loser' and 'Guardian Soulmates'. Although I say I will, my heart's not in it, let alone my soul, mate.

The question of whether to rekindle Arnold comes up, but goes straight back down again.

On a lighter note, Blondie keeps us in fits with her ongoing Senior Citizen Kane saga. She confides that he needed worryingly high doses of Viagra. Once, when she simply couldn't bear another 'Aren't I virile?' session, she stole it from the bedroom cabinet and hid it. Despite this precaution he appeared in the kitchen an hour later, naked as a peeled banana and sporting a raging hard-on. She looked him up and down, said, 'Oh, that looks like an erect penis only smaller,' and went back to reading her *Daily Mail*. He shuffled out and moments later she heard strange spanking noises coming from the bathroom.

'I assumed he was beating the wretched thing down with the back of a slipper,' Blondie tells her wide-eyed audience and we all dissolve into fits of giggles.

Now I don't want you thinking that all my single girlfriends and I ever talk about is men, men and men; but you have to admit, it's a pretty big topic. Since we're all living so much longer and are physically active well into our sixties and beyond, filling our free time has to include consorting with the opposite sex. Caring for children, grandchildren and ageing parents, as well as maintaining careers, homes and friendships are all important and energy consuming activities. However for women like us, there's always room for love, no matter how old you get.

The argument that partnership with a person of one's own age is a kinder way to 'go gently into that good night' is beaten at me like a drum. Yes, I understand this would be a less challenging option but I still cannot picture myself doing it. I see myself walking a high wire, or slithering in a snake pit; no hand-in-hand stroll into the sunset for the likes of me. You see, I'd rather eat one lavish meal then starve, than have the security of bread for the rest of my life. As someone once said, '(Wo)man cannot live by bread alone.'

Although the girls are concerned about me getting hurt and try their damnedest to steer me safely past the rocks, I also believe that they actually enjoy the *schadenfreude* provided by my stories; they get a vicarious thrill as they hear about the ups and downs of a life so fully lived. I feel it my duty to keep them entertained, so entertain them I must. It's a filthy job but someone has to do it.

♀

By the time Thursday comes around, I've got my act together sufficiently to face the outside world again. I have a late business appointment with a rather camp Austrian art dealer I met recently while researching current values of 1950s furniture. When I first set eyes on him, I noted how attractive he was, but dismissed this as irrelevant because at the time I Had A Boyfriend. I was also sure that he (the Austrian, not the boyfriend) was probably gay. I turned out to be wrong – on both counts.

Friedrich von Eurotrash is perma-tanned, with very blue, very piercing, very *fuck-me* eyes. He is of medium height, slim and suave with luxuriant chestnut-brown hair curling at the nape of his neck; hair that makes you want to run your fingers through it. Eurotrash shakes me by the hand then kisses me several times on each cheek. He then swans around his gallery flamboyantly showing off his 'conceptual room settings' and returns to his desk to hunt for a rather rare art book useful for my research. He then closes the gallery and invites me for a drink at the Electric Brasserie in Notting Hill.

No sooner are we seated than the conversation turns to personal stuff. He tells me that like me he's twice divorced and has four children. Presumably not gay, then.

He orders another round of very strong, very spicy Bloody Marys when we're only halfway through the first lot. This second drink's an aberration: a bloody Tabasco cocktail with a dash of terrified virgin thrown in. My first sip goes down like lava but I tough it out, barely managing to control my larynx without coughing my kidneys up into my hand. The fiery vodka does its evil work though, loosening my tongue sufficiently to the point that the confidences we share suggest that sex will follow.

We order dinner and by the time the Seafood Platter for Two arrives, he's stroking my arm and running his well-heeled Teutonic boot up and down my leg. I can't pretend I'm not enjoying this but for some reason, I feel slightly guilty. What can I say? Jews do Guilt like Debbie does Dallas.

I pick up the shellfish crackers and prise open the lobster claws, sliding them out of their coral curves and feeding them onto his plate. He slurps a couple of oysters with his eyes locked on mine, and the inference of his tongue savouring the slippery mollusc leaves little to the imagination.

The Electric is becoming too noisy to maintain our conversation, so he pays the bill and invites me for a nightcap at a moody little dive nearby. Thursday being the new Saturday, the place is heaving and we are obliged to stand rammed up against each other at the bar.

Already three sheets to the wind, I order a Mojito and much to the barman's annoyance, help myself to a pomegranate from behind the counter, which I split open with my thumbnail and feed to Eurotrash, seed by juicy seed. He is now stroking my inner thigh up to my armpit, whispering in my ear how much he would like to eat the pomegranate from my belly button. My tart-o-meter emits a loud ping.

Eurotrash walks me to my car and offers to follow me home on his pimped-up Piaggio scooter. Self-preservation kicks in and I manage to decline. He'll keep. But will I? I know it's only been a week but love is a like a violin and if I don't keep practising, I'll forget how to play.

At 03.55 I am woken by a text. It's Eurotrash, obviously trashed:
God, he writes. *I wish you would be next to me right now...x*

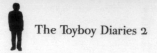

Fucking men! It's always about them, isn't it? But I smile because somebody wants me, then I turn over and go back to sleep.

Fifteen

One evening soon after, Blondie calls me with the news that she's got a date with the man who broke her heart a few years ago. Senior Citizen Kane is failing to amuse her on all counts and in any case, sex with an ex doesn't count as infidelity, does it?

'Why go there again?' I ask as if I didn't know.

'Pot, kettle, black, darling,' she says tartly, which needs no explanation.

I enjoy the diversion of someone else's traumas for a change. Recently, I've been far too bogged down in my own.

During the afternoon of this regressive event, she calls me several times:

'What shall I wear? Skirt or trousers? Boots or shoes? Shirt or top?'

'If I wear big knickers, then I won't be tempted, will I?'

'If I don't drink alcohol, then I won't be tempted, will I?'

'If I don't get waxed, then I won't be tempted, will I?'

We agree that once men reach that general area, they don't notice a few stray hairs anyway. (They do notice if you're bare as a baby though, like my old flame Benjamin when he slithered down to discover my first Hollywood. 'You exquisite bitch!' he exclaimed, and didn't surface till I dragged him up by the ears.)

Blondie calls again at 6 p.m. He's not picking her up till 8. She's done her hair and make-up and is pacing the floor in her underwear still wondering what to wear.

'Sounds like you're ready to roll to me,' I comment sardonically.

'Don't be ridiculous!' she laughs. 'This is overdressed! I used to greet him at the door with rouged nipples beneath a see-through shirt wearing stilettos and hold-ups with no knickers.'

'Hmmm . . . ' I muse. 'Men like that don't come around much any more.'

'I'm scared, Wend,' she says. 'I'm really scared.'

'Then don't do this!' I may as well tell her not to scratch an itch.

'What are you talking about?' she objects. 'Of course I have to do it! I never really got over him. I need to meet him, find him revolting and then at last I'll get closure!'

Ah, closure. Such an elusive element. It allows the mind to find clarity, the soul to find peace, the body to re-energize itself and the heart to stop regretting. We all want closure. What we get instead is angst, regret, recrimination, torment, sorrow, despair and homicide. Closure is just great – if you can get it.

The next day, a different girlfriend (not one with my best interests at heart!) links me to a new website called toyboywarehouse. com and before I know it, the devil's taken over my keyboard and posted up my profile knocking ten years off my age. (You might want to remember this, it's relevant later on!) Within minutes, a whole kennel-full of waggy tailed little puppies come sniffing round my inbox.

After losing a couple of precious hours on this addictive waste of time, I get my head together sufficiently to do some work. However temptation has winked at me from across a crowded room and over the next few days, I dip in and out like it's my favourite candy store. I can shop for a chocolate flake, aniseed balls or a big pink gobstopper without leaving the comfort of my own home.

One of the guys is an aspirant porn writer and tries his efforts out on me:

I dreamt about you last night. I came into your room, crept beneath the duvet and went down on you for hours. You tore at my hair begging me not to stop as your body wriggled uncontrollably and your legs wrapped themselves tighter and tighter around my head. You were so wet you couldn't take it any more so you pulled me up alongside you and ran your hands over my strong shoulders before licking the smooth skin on the side of my neck. I moved to start touching myself but you wouldn't let me. Even though I was rock hard and desperate for you to stroke me, you made me wait . . .

Another less intense one tempts me out with, *Hiya pretty lady! Fancy meeting up for a drink this weekend?* He seems fairly innocuous and his photo shows a very cute face. Nevertheless I am about to log off – no more toyboys, no more men, remember? – when suddenly an old adage springs to mind; one that has stood me in good stead before now. It goes: *the best way to get over one man is to get under another* so, under this banner, I accept.

In the evening I go to a gig with Rock Chick at the Hope & Anchor in Upper Street. Her son JB is playing again. I can only assume that MLP isn't going to be there. Probably snogging his new girl-friend in a car park off the Old Kent Road surrounded by empty beer cans and burger wrappers. I know that sounded Meeow! But the truth is, I've had my share of heart-rending moments *vis à vis* MLP. It's just that I try not to mention them.

During the evening I exchange another few texts with Cute Face. He obviously fancies himself as a bit of a comedian because when I tell him I'm at a gig, he comments: *You're really quite trendy for someone who grew up in Victorian times, aren't you?*

I am affronted at his effrontery. He better not say anything ageist to my face. That would be very dangerous. I tell him to *watch it or you're gonna get a smack* and then, just to show there are no hard feelings, I end with, *I must go now and boil the milk for my cocoa.*

He then sends me a text obviously meant for someone else: *No mate, she doesn't seem nuts. Looks well pretty actually. I'll just see how it goes.*

Thank God he didn't say anything derogatory. I'm amused by the 'nuts' comment though. He may not think so, but personally, I'm convinced of it.

I call him on my way home and we have a long chat. He makes me roar with laughter, which is something I haven't done for too long a time. This has a very positive effect on me and lifts my spirits enormously. If he's as cute as he is entertaining, our date on Saturday should be good fun. I've told him if he behaves himself, I might invite him back to mine to watch the Eurovision Song Contest. What a lure!

He continues texting me till way past midnight, the messages getting dirtier and more overt. I know exactly what he's up to . . . they're all the same once they start thinking horizontally.

♀

On Saturday my boisterous little granddaughters come for lunch, and in the afternoon we go to blow off steam in the park. They're wearing their wheelie trainers so I take along a pair of ski poles and tuck one under each arm telling them to grab the ends. Then I begin to jog, dragging them behind me whooping and screaming as if I'm a horse and they're the cart. After a circuit around the perimeter I collapse onto the grass exhausted, thinking how blessed I am to have these darling children in my life. This is what reality is made of – not hankering after some age-inappropriate brain fuck that brings me more grief than relief.

We go back to my flat and the girlies do some painting, play Jenga, have a dollies' tea party, make a general mess, grow tired and go home. I tidy up and get ready for the evening.

At 7.30 p.m. I drive to the station and park where I can see the exit. Cute Face (I assume it is he) arrives on time and I see him clocking another woman with a look of fear in his eyes. She's a bit of a minger and I can tell by his about-to-leg-it body language that he thinks it might be me.

I bound out of the car and appear at his side and his relief is evident. He hugs me hello and hands me a carrier bag. Inside is a bottle of Taittinger. When he texted this morning to ask if I preferred red or white, I told him to surprise me. He did.

It's a fine evening so we drive down to the Waterway on Little Venice for a couple of drinks. He's fun and I feel safe with him so we go home as planned to watch Eurovision. I used this invitation in a post-modern ironic way but I've made a mistake. It's not on for another couple of weeks. Oh well . . .

I put out some nibbles and we set about getting consummately trashed. We drink the champagne and once we've finished that, I liberate some peach and raspberry schnapps shots from the freezer. He then decides to concoct a cocktail into which he throws a toxic mix of rum, vodka, amaretto, brandy and fruit juice. For someone who doesn't drink much, I'm a very boozy floozy.

I put some Bon Jovi on and we air-guitar around the living room in what we think is dancing but which is more like crashing into things. This isn't big and it isn't clever. Both my furniture and I bruise easily.

Without asking, he then raids my fridge and opens the nice, cold bottle of Moët I'd been saving for a special occasion. Might this be it? We toss the bottle back and forth between us, spilling a fair amount on the carpet and the sofa. Then, horribly and suddenly, I think I'm going to be sick and rush to the loo. Thank God the nausea passes, and I lurch back into the living room and change the CD to the Pointer Sisters. The neighbours will surely appreciate our authenticity as we obey the order to *Jump!*

At around 11 p.m., having had no dinner and enough alcohol to strip the Forth Bridge, we stagger like drunken sailors into the bedroom where we embark on an orgy of unrestrained sex. I can't remember the finer details except to say I really enjoyed it and it went on for a very long time. Aren't young men wonderful?! Apart from a Cute Face this one has a Cute Smile, Cute Body, Cute Bum . . . and a Huge Dick.

When *my body's had enough of him and I'm lying flat out on the floor,* he makes love to me again and this continues until about 5 a.m. when I tell him to leave me the hell alone so I can get some sleep.

He snores like Darth Vader with a bronchial problem but I stuff my earplugs in and when the room stops spinning, I eventually close my eyes.

We make love again between 8 a.m. and midday, then I get up v-e-r-y s-l-o-w-l-y and cook us a full English breakfast.

Later that morning he showers, gets dressed, hugs me affectionately and leaves to watch the football – but not before making a date for two Saturdays hence to watch Eurovision. Again.

I stagger around the flat like a robot whose batteries are running down. I need to make a Bolognese because the grandchildren are coming over for lunch and the place looks like the day after Glastonbury, though thankfully without the mud. I find my bra in the fireplace and my knickers in the fridge. How the hell did they get there? I don't remember being that drunk! Imagine if I hadn't found them and one of the kids had? I'd have had to make up some excuse, but what? *Didi likes her panties cold because . . . because . . .* I give up. My brain's barely firing on one cylinder, never mind stretching to elaborate excuses. I bury the empties at the bottom of a bin bag and run myself a bath.

Lying in the comfort of the ylang-ylang infused water, I hear my phone go off. One certainty in life, apart from death and taxes, is that your phone will always ring when you're in the bath or on the pot. I wipe my hands and reach for it.

It's Cute Face to say what a great time he's had. Aaah! Sweet. A few minutes later it goes off again. It's a multi-media message with a picture of his hand grasping the engorged base of his fully erect penis. I'm shocked but not offended – after all, I saw it in person not an hour ago. I'm a bit surprised though that it isn't nesting quietly against his inner thigh considering the night it's

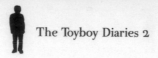

had, and am further taken aback by his next missive which is a live video clip of him pleasuring himself.

Lovely.

Thanks for sharing.

I can hardly walk and he's having a wank the minute he's gets home? Or at least, I *presume* he's at home and not loitering by the bus stop on the Edgware Road. My tender nethers feel the urgent need to convalesce, but look at this young 'un go!

I text him to stop being a *dirty, little bugger* then carry on with my day, marvelling as I go at the unpredictability of my love life.

Sixteen

By the following Wednesday, my weekend high has slumped to a mid-week low. Cute Face was fine as far as he went but I miss MLP terribly. I seem unable to console myself with my usual sanctuaries of work, family and friends. Like a flower craves water, male attention is my drug.

I fool around a while on toyboywarehouse.com and get chatting to a certain Arrogant Rugby Player (ARP). He tells me that when we meet he's going to 'rock my world'. Yes . . . well . . . whatever . . . I've just had my world rocked by someone else, thank you very much, and I'm still wobbling. ARP wastes no time inviting me away for a long weekend to a Country House Hotel – somewhere he knows with 'roaming peacocks and awesome rooms'. I tell him cheekily that I prefer 'awesome peacocks and roaming rooms' so he calls me a 'smart arse – the cockiest woman I know'. I thank him for the compliment. He then suggests taking me shopping for an 'expensive cocktail dress'. The word 'cock', in one form or another, features heavily in his conversation.

On Friday, in a bid to keep the mood upbeat, I decide to give Eurotrash a further run for his money.

I time my visit deliberately late in the day and the minute I walk into the gallery he's all over me like cling film. By fortuitous coincidence, he has to deliver a quirky lamp to a client near to where I live. We set off in tandem then go for a drink, which turns into a second and then a third.

It's a beautiful evening and we sit in the patio garden outside Le Cochonnet near Little Venice. Eurotrash is very easy company, commenting irreverently on all the passers-by in a strong, Austro-Hungarian accent that makes me giggle. Although I know he's a wrong 'un, somehow we fit.

He tells me about an Indian production of *A Midsummer Night's Dream* he saw at The Roundhouse recently and complains that he couldn't follow the plot. I remember a book I have at home called *Shakespeare for Idiots* and, as I live just over the road, I invite him back to borrow it.

As you might expect, the Bard is forgotten the minute we walk in the door. Eurotrash chases me frivolously from room to room and before I know it, I'm running a bubble bath, lighting candles, opening a bottle, searching for ciggies and selecting music. Drunk and disorderly, we slide into the warm tub where we slither all over each other like a merman and his maid.

Eurotrash is sporting an impressive organ that pokes out of the water like a peniscope. The invitation is irresistible and I lower my head and sink my lips around it. He groans appreciatively and massages my feet.

We finish the wine and talk and laugh and it feels like someone's changed the fuse in me and twiddled the right knobs. Normal service has been resumed.

We emerge from the bath and step naked onto the terrace just off my bedroom. The night is mild and torpid and he wraps his arms around me and pulls me back against him, bending his knees as he tries to enter me.

I'm not so drunk that I don't know that there's no way I'm having full, penetrative, unsafe sex with Eurotrash, tonight or any other night. I remind myself I currently have a 'lover' though frankly, a one-night-stand with Cute Face does not a romance make.

Eurotrash takes my rejection with good grace. When he leaves, we're still laughing and still horny. No mental anguish is involved, no demands, no commitment. He promises to come over again soon. He says he'd like to 'cook a crispy duck' – or it might have been 'book a crazy fuck'. Either way, it's fine by me.

My flirtation with Arrogant Rugby Player continues apace. He requests my address as he says he has 'a special gift' to send me. I presume it's going to come with batteries but I'm pleasantly surprised when a little box arrives from Myla containing a beautiful set of écru lace lingerie. I thank him kindly for the bra and pants but comment that their purchase does not guarantee him access to the contents once I'm wearing them.

Cute Face continues to textually harass me throughout the week. On the Thursday, I suggest that he may want to come shopping with me on Eurovision Saturday to buy a new TV. You'd have thought I'd offered him a shared stateroom on a first-class cruise liner with the newly crowned Miss Universe and her twin sister. *God you really know how to get a man going! Electronics shopping . . . absolutely!! Bring it on x*

He then goes on to recommend a 72" Flat-Screen Edge-Lit LED-based LCD Surround-Sound Wireless VHRAM Home Cinema. I tell him I just need a new TV. All he has to do is put it in the car, carry it up three flights of stairs and install it. Then he can teach the Victorian woman how it works. Then I might make him a cup of tea.

The only reward I want . . . he answers . . . *is to ravish your sexy naked body.* (You don't get *that* at John Lewis, no matter how Never Knowingly Undersold they are.)

Now some people might question the fact that a 27-year-old is complimenting a 62-year-old on her 'sexy naked body', but as Marcus Antonius pointed out when he seduced Cleopatra away from Julius Caesar, *Penis erectus non habet conscientiam.* In any case, I have it on good authority (yoga teacher, unforgiving mirror, ex-lovers who come back for more) that my form's not bad. And no one's ever asked for their money back. And frankly, when a man's lust has risen, it doesn't really matter if you're Scarlett Johanssen or a watermelon.

Friday. The day begins with a courteous Good Morning message:

I can't get rid of my raging horn. You must have warped me, Salisbury, and degenerates into such poetic phrases as:

I wish I had my tongue in your pussy right now . . .

I'm absolutely longing to fuck you any way you want me . . .

Can't wait to feel you cum on my rock hard cock . . .

This not-unwelcome barrage of texts reminds me of the early days with MLP when it was all full on and brimming with pent-up passion – except *he* was never quite *that* rude.

In the afternoon I go to the Torture Chamber and have a Holly-wood. I'd broached the subject of depilation with Cute Face last weekend and he told me to surprise him. I surprise myself by managing not to scream.

I hope you like 12 yr olds . . . I text him, when I've stopped smarting.

Cool, he replies immediately, *I'll be giving you a good tongue lashing tomorrow.*

A little later, having pondered the matter at length, he asks:

So when you get a waxing, do you have to get naked?

How else? I reply. *What are you thinking about? Another woman touching my cho-cho?*

I wasn't . . . but I am now. Have you ever done that? Not that I'm asking . . . you're more than enough for little old me but I bet you have, being the experienced woman you are.

I decide not to rise to this challenge. It's for me to know and him to find out.

The next morning I awake to a drunken voice message left in the early hours by Cute Face. I hear the noise of his feet crunching along a road. Then comes his voice slurring, *I'm really looking forward to seeing you tomorrow . . . hic . . . bye-byebyebye . . .* followed by the sound of someone tripping, then a thud and a groan.

At 10.15 a.m. I text him a mischievous and perky *good morning! x* and an hour later, he gets back with, *not feelin gr8.*

I reply rather curtly: *There's a surprise . . . Can you please come at 3.30 so we can go and buy the TV?* but I don't hear back.

I'm not unduly worried.

Well maybe just a little.

Cute Face arrives around 3 p.m. He's only 5'7". I'm only 5'3" and I rarely wear high heels at home unless I'm trying to seduce someone. Since he's already been suitably seduced, today I'm barefoot.

When he hugs me at the door, this makes him sufficiently taller than me for his stature not to matter to either of us.

He has bright blue eyes with long lashes and curly fair hair. There's an impish air about him, like a naughty boy who's just about to get naughtier. His Saturday stubble adds a roguish edge.

Because it's too early for alcohol, I go and put the kettle on and the afternoon turns into a Victorian tea party. I set the tray with an embroidered cloth, decant the jam into a china ramekin, grill then butter the crumpets, slice the cake and lay the entire feast in front of him. He switches the (old) TV on (I've made him far too comfortable to contemplate going out to buy a new one this afternoon) and we relax on the sofa in each other's arms. It's only 3.20 p.m. We have all the time in the world . . .

By 3.23 p.m. we're rolling around on the floor with our heads between each other's legs. He yanks off the Myla underwear I'm wearing (well, I wasn't going to waste it and God knows when I'll meet ARP) and delights in my Hollywood. He has reciprocated by shaving his entire genitalia, so we're as silky smooth as the babes in the wood.

When we finish Round One, we return to the fireside for more tea and a game of Scrabble. He says he's never played before but he picks it up bloody quickly and tries to thrash me. I can see the signs of a very bad loser coming out and I don't wish to antagonize him this early in the weekend.

We finish two points short of each other, but he only won due to my expert tuition. To celebrate his victory, I give him a blow job which leads back to bed for Round Two.

At 6 p.m., he pours us both a Scotch and ginger and I cut up some crudités to eat with the blue-cheese dip I prepared earlier. We relax back on the sofa, cuddled up in each other's arms. The stars

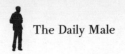

seem aligned in perfect symmetry. At 8 p.m. I stick an M&S Thai in the oven and we eat it off a tray in front of the (not likely to be renewed at the moment) TV. Aaaah! Blissto.

Having started our date at 3.30 p.m. and worked pretty hard all afternoon, by 10 p.m. we're both shattered. The unspeakable caterwauling of various Eurovision contestants has proved even more exhausting. He falls asleep spooned in behind me, snoring like a warthog. I tolerate this for as long as I am able, then I get up and clear away the dinner things. When I return to the living room, he's still passed out, one leg over the back of the sofa, his face buried in a pile of pillows. The snoring continues apace, so I switch off the lights, lower the volume on the TV and get ready for bed. I contemplate throwing a duvet over him (déjà vu? déjà duvet?) but I don't want to wake him, so I adjust the heating and slide happily into bed on my own.

Around 2 a.m. I hear him get up to go the loo and then, of course, he comes to join me. Blast! He snuggles up and starts poking his ramrod around the general buttock area but I ignore him. He soon falls asleep again with his face pressed hard against the back of my neck. The snoring reprises in earnest and I push him away crossly and reach for my earplugs. Unconscious still but bellowing like a bull surrounded by nubile young heifers, he spread-eagles himself across the bed then thrashes around for what's left of the night.

By 6 a.m. I'm wide-awake and grumpy. God – the price one has to pay for a couple of orgasms. (Hail, oh Rabbit! I love thee well). I can't say I'm devastated when he leaves. I have a feeling that this little fling has possibly been flung.

♀

The wedding is only a week away and the atmosphere is definitely hotting up. Everything seems to be in place but I still get the odd panic-stricken phone call from my fraught and frantic daughter. I calm, cajole and reassure her while wincing at the deafening sound of plastic being pushed repeatedly into credit card machines.

It's a relief when Wednesday comes around and, along with it, my monthly get-together with the Sisterhood.

We all go to Calm's house for dinner. She's made a Thai fish curry in coconut cream sauce, served in a hollowed-out pineapple shell, which is so delicious that chewing the fat is exchanged for savouring the stew.

As we clear away the plates and settle down for a good old natter, Blondie fills us in on her closure-seeking reunion with her erstwhile ex. It gave her neither pleasure nor closure, it seems.

'God, I hate men,' she groans theatrically, yet again. 'But at least I got to re-open an aperture that was threatening to close, if you know what I mean!'

'And what about you, Wend?' she asks, turning to me. 'How was your weekend with The Cute One?'

'It was fine,' I tell her.

'Only fine?' asks Calm in surprise. 'That doesn't sound too enamoured.'

I shrug. 'He came over, I made tea, we had sex, I made more tea, we had more sex, he fell asleep, he woke up, we had sex again, we played Scrabble, we ate dinner, we had sex, we – ' I hold up my hand to correct myself – '*he* went to sleep and snored like a donkey being fed through a sausage grinder, we had sex, I made breakfast, he went home. What can I tell you?'

'How do you cope with all that shared intimacy leading to nothing?' queries Sensible, leaning so intently across the table that her silk shirt soaks up the remains of her raspberry coulis. My need to reply is delayed by her squeal of horror and the conversation is hurriedly diverted to a barrage of How To advice on stain removal.

'Hand-wash it,' says Half Empty.

'That dry-clean spray works quite well,' advises Blondie.

'It'll have to be Jeeves, I'm afraid,' moans Sensible, 'which'll cost nearly as much as the shirt itself!'

She gives me an accusatory look as if my nefarious love life was directly responsible for her sartorial misfortune.

'So, how *do* you cope?' Sensible asks eventually, picking up the thread of her previous interrogation.

'It's the name of the game – the one I play at any rate,' I answer.

'But sweetie – ' she begins again, then catches Calm's eye and bites her lip.

'Actually, I don't know how I cope,' I go on pensively, not really wanting to address this issue for much longer. 'I try not to get too attached, I guess . . . but I don't always succeed.'

'At least you've got over your *previous* toyboy, haven't you?' says Half Empty, hoping for my sake that this is true.

'Well, not exactly,' I reply. 'But I'm managing to . . . er . . . fill the gap . . . '

'Taken up Bridge yet, that's right?' asks Sensible, nodding at me encouragingly.

'A bridge too far!' I say, but I'm the only one smiling. I notice Calm doing that 'non-judgmental' thing over the top of her glasses that makes me feel like I'm in the dock for manslaughter.

'Yes?' I ask her.

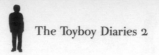

'Strikes me you could do with a break,' she points out.

'From what?' I say innocently.

'Your mission to self-destruct?'

'I've got a little wedding coming up!' I remind her.

'You'll need a holiday after,' Half Empty assures me. 'When my daughter got married, I crashed out at a health farm for two whole weeks.'

'A little escapade to the mountains, perhaps? Replace all those toxins with some clean, fresh air?' urges Calm.

'Sounds divine!' I nod enthusiastically. 'Oh thank you! I feel better already!'

And we agree to book a ski trip as soon as we are able.

Seventeen

The night before Lily's wedding!

A gaggle of girls spills up the stairs for a Mother Hen Night (the Spring Chicks party took place two weeks ago and crinklies were *not* invited.) My sister and her family have arrived from Spain and there is much hugging and kissing as all the cousins reunite. The decibel-level of fifteen females rises in proportion to the champagne consumed, though I try to cap this at one glass per head to avoid hangovers in the morning. I want everyone to look and feel their best.

Calm and Sensible enter bearing an amazing tropical fruit arrangement the size of a small Caribbean island. There are chunks of mango, papaya, lychees and rambutan all adorned with chocolate-covered strawberries. The girls make a beeline for the latter – women + chocolate = mmmmm! as everybody knows.

Lily glows her way through the evening wearing an *I'm the Bride* sash with flashing lights on it. We end the soirée early with a raucous rendition of 'I'm getting married in the morning,' and everyone trots off to their respective beds.

Lily is sleeping *chez moi* in her old room tonight. We get

into our nighties and I make us two mugs of warm Nesquik. Then she climbs sleepily into her old bed. I go to tuck her in and, because I know it's unlikely I'll ever have the chance again, I pull her childhood copy of *When We Were Very Young* down from the shelf. I sit on the edge of her bed and open it. Lily smiles dreamily at me and the years just slip away. I turn to her favourite poem, *The King's Breakfast*, which I read to her just as I did when *she* was very young. Her thumb slips into her mouth as she listens. Her eyelids droop and I close the book quietly. I stroke her cheek and kiss her forehead as I fight back the tears. Tomorrow my little Miss will become a Mrs. All I can do is hope that she and her new husband are blessed with love throughout their lives.

The next morning, we set off early to the hairdresser then return home for scrambled eggs and smoked salmon accompanied by a glass of Buck's Fizz.

We gather our clothes, shoes, make-up and overnight bags and I surprise Lily when a white Rolls Royce, bedecked with ribbons, arrives to drive us to the heart of the city. The weather has also blessed us: it's bright and beautiful; the sky is blue, the heavens are clear.

We are bursting with excitement as the car arrives at the Great Eastern Hotel where we spread ourselves out in the luxury suite offered as part of the wedding package. Throughout the day people pop in and out to wish her luck: the bridesmaids, members of our respective families, in-laws, outlaws, room service, photographers, florists, videographers.

At 3.00 p.m. we close the doors and start to get ready for the main event.

Lily does her own make-up as do I; then I help her into her wedding dress. I recall doing this for Poppy in the bedroom of my first husband and his second wife's house. It's a truly memorable experience – a tense yet tender bonding between mother and daughter when all previous fractures are forgotten in the unique pleasure of a magic moment. No matter how old the bride is – Poppy was 24 and Lily is 31 – she's still your little girl and seeing her in her wedding gown, knowing she is leaving you to give her life to another, is incredibly emotional.

Lily steps carefully into the tiered organza skirt and boned satin top, and with practiced diligence I draw the ribbons together at the back of the *bustier*. I must ensure they are tight enough for it to fit her properly but loose enough so she can still breathe *and* sit down. An unobtrusive photographer records our every move.

When she is satisfied and comfortable, I slip her feet into her ivory satin wedding shoes and kneel to fasten the ankle straps. I'm relieved that the Mayan ankle tattoo she had done during her year in Guatemala hardly shows beneath the glitzy bridal tights! Last of all, with trembling fingers, I secure the pearls my mother gave Lily for her 21st birthday around her flawless neck. Then I stand back to observe the picture.

She looks as I always knew she would: simply beautiful.

I fight back the tears so as not to ruin my make-up. There have been so many lumps in my throat recently I'm not sure I'm going to make it through the day without blubbing. I take a few deep breaths and compose myself. The photographer snaps me unawares and I smile broadly, but when I catch sight of myself in the mirror I wish I'd had some filler put in those laugh lines after all. I make a mental note to treat myself once my empty coffers have been replenished.

Just then my second ex-husband, Lily's father, knocks and enters. He gasps when he sees his daughter in her gown and his eyes well up. We all hug – a family united once again. I affix the corsage to his lapel and ask if he's OK. He nods uncertainly. I know how he feels. We grew apart as husband and wife, but we've always been there, together as friends, for our daughter.

Other family members flurry in and out: my mother and my lovely Aunty Betty; my sister and her family; Poppy and the darling little bridesmaids dressed as flower fairies. They hold wands made of rosebuds and floral coronas encircle their waist-length hair. They prance about in their sparkly shoes sprinkling stardust everywhere, like two nymphs in a woodland glade.

I hand Lily her lily bouquet and look at my watch. As if summoned by the nervous gesture, the wedding coordinator appears at the door.

'You all look so glamorous!' she exclaims. 'Now Lily,' she says to my nervous little girl, 'it's time to go.'

We take the lift down to the wood-panelled drawing room where the ceremony will take place. Rows of chairs covered in ivory satin fabric adorned with bows are crammed with family and friends. The atmosphere is electric, the anticipation palpable.

The room grows quiet as the procession begins. My other son-in-law walks me down the aisle between the twinkling pillar candles and statuesque vases of fresh and fragrant blooms. I take my seat in the front row and a silence descends as the guests hold their breath. The guitarist strums the opening chords of *El Concierto de Aranjuez,* and Lily glides in, quivering gently on her father's arm.

Her face is a picture of happiness and disbelief that this moment has finally arrived. She appears to be laughing and crying all at once. The groom turns and sees his bride shimmering

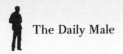

down the aisle towards him. The smile they exchange could melt a marble heart.

The rest of the evening goes off perfectly in a blur of pink champagne and canapés, photos and videos, dinner and dancing, wedding cake and speeches, love and happiness and much merriment.

To see the excitement in the young couple's eyes fills me with joy and even if I'm never loved again, at least I know that Lily is from this day forth forever more.

Having so much to do in the run-up to the wedding kept my mind from straying to the dark side. Maybe I should become a wedding planner, I think to myself ruefully as I put away my dress and shoes the next day. I could get my kicks from the vicarious thrill of other people's romances instead of beating my brains out over my own. Now it is all over, though, I experience a sense of loss. I think gratefully about the foresight of my friends, who knew how I'd feel.

And so it is that a few days later, Calm Best Friend and I set off on our impulsive ski trip.

Eighteen

Calm Best Friend and I reach the check-in desk at the crack of stupid o'clock. Despite the earliness of the hour, we can't help noticing the handsome older man sporting the same luggage tags as us who is standing next in line. This is a singles ski trip – we will be forty in all – and he's clearly part of our group. Yippee! Handsome Older Man (HOM – isn't that a make of boxer shorts?) and I make fleeting eye contact but I look away swiftly and decide to let CBF have first dibs. There are several reasons for this:

a) I don't need another involvement just now

b) she hasn't had a boyfriend for a while

c) I don't need another involvement just now, and

d) I'm tired and I keep repeating myself.

After the flight to Geneva and a seemingly endless four-hour coach journey to Val d'Isère, we arrive at the resort. Here we are welcomed by Eric (or 'Eh-reek' as he calls himself), the Club Med *Chef de Village*. Eh-reek is tall, tanned, suave and sexy – a badass Frenchman if ever I saw one. He has a 'You're next!' look in his eye and I wouldn't trust him further than I could toss him. What a time he must have seducing all those vulnerable lady guests, I think with a knowing smile. He'd be wading knee-deep through thermal knickers by the end of every day.

CBF is very taken with Hot Frog but *I* wouldn't touch him with a sterilized bargepole. It's too clichéd anyway, like shagging the tennis coach or the ski instructor.

He is rather tasty though.

Calm and I awake the next morning in Alpine heaven. After a night-long dump of snow, the weather is picture perfect. We ski all day, filling our London lungs with fresh mountain air, then swish down the slopes at sunset to find Hot Frog and his team of G.O.s ready to greet us.

For the Club Med uninitiated, G.O.s are the *Gentils Organisateurs* or 'Gracious Organisers' who provide service and entertainment round the clock. They're dressed in Rio Carnival attire today, dispensing smiles and chit-chat as they serve the skiers mulled wine, hot drinks and a selection of freshly baked cakes.

I help myself to a dark, moist chocolate brownie and a glass of *vin chaud* and go into raptures, in French of course, as I savour the orgasmic flavours. I notice Hot Frog listening to me but I pretend indifference. Eventually he wanders over and asks me where I'm from. I tell him I'm English but I went to the Lycée Français and a lively dialogue ensues. He's very complimentary about my accent and of course, the more he flatters, the more I show off. He tells me he's half French, half Spanish, which is an irresistible cue for me to change idioms. Isn't education a wonderful thing? The trouble is that although I speak four languages, I can't say 'no' in any of them.

Calm and I finish our snack then sashay away to get ready for the evening – as best one can when dressed in puffy ski suits and enormous plastic boots. I glance back somewhat coyly to see Hot Frog watching us. His jade-green eyes scan me up and down and I surreptitiously check my ankles to make sure he hasn't severed my knicker elastic with the power of his laser-like gaze. Jeepers Creepers! Where *did* he get those peepers? A little frisson fizzles through me but I douse it immediately with a bucketful of snow-cold thoughts.

The holiday progresses with a swing – or rather a swoosh and a swish. Calm and I spend the first couple of days skiing and our evenings socializing with the rest of the group. They're a good crowd once we get to know them. The free-flowing wine and generous cocktails over dinner help forge new friendships and I pause to reflect gratefully that my sadness over MLP is lessening by the minute.

By the third day, I have developed a warm friendship with the Handsome Older Man from the check-in desk at the airport. He turns out to be quick-witted and very clever. He's almost 47, a set designer, has never been married and lives quite close to me in London. He's also nice-looking and extremely charismatic. There is a distinct mental chemistry between us, and I strive to match him in both wit and wisdom. I find myself thinking, rather wist-fully, that with God and Eros on my side he could really qualify as The Right Man. Younger than me but old enough. And wouldn't my friends be pleased? But I dismiss the thought with a shrug, telling myself that he's not the kind of man I normally go for and he probably doesn't like me *like that* anyway.

On day three, Calm and I discover the most fabulous restaurant on the slopes, which we make for each day at one o'clock. There's fresh food, live music and ice-cold bottles of champagne chilling in the snow around the bar. We're beginning to ski like Jewish Princesses: late lift up, one run down for a very long lunch then the slow slope home.

'This is the life,' I say to Calm as we tuck into a cheese fondue washed down with a glass of sparkling rosé. 'Who needs men? They're only aggravation.'

She nods, spearing another bread cube with her fork and swirling it round in the melted cheese. 'And if they're old they're *viagravation!*' We fall about laughing. There's something heady about alcohol and altitude that makes us giggle like liberated schoolgirls.

I take a wrong turn that afternoon and end up by myself on a black run. Clumping into the Piste Bar at sunset, I hope my wet bottom doesn't advertise the fact that I had a spectacular wipe-out. I head shakily for the steaming vat of mulled wine, grateful that I made it back in one piece. I haven't had to come down the mountain on the Blood Wagon yet, and I hope I never do.

Hot Frog is serving the drinks and we chat for a while before he draws me aside into a private conversation. Leaning close and dropping his voice to a whisper, he asks me why my husband has let me come on holiday without him. Men are so transparent – except when they're being dense, of course. I tell him I murdered my last two husbands and now have a stable of young studs at my beck and call. Honesty and modesty are not my strongest virtues, but then neither is this inaccuracy a million miles from the truth.

I'm not consciously aware of giving him the come-on, but suddenly he moulds his mouth around my ear and asks if I'd like to meet him at midnight for a drink, after the floor show ends.

You could have knocked me down with a snowflake! My earlier dismissal of him as obvious and clichéd is swept away by the avalanche of his audacious advances. I shrug one shoulder, smile coquettishly, adopt my best Brigitte Bardot pout and reply, *'Peut être'*, before slithering away to the boot room. My heart is thumping and my mouth is dry, but somehow I manage not to break my neck on the ice in my distracted state. How the hell did *that* happen? I've come away to rest and regroup, and here I am accepting a late-night date!

I wriggle out of my boots and hurry off down the hall feeling fluttery yet elated. I don't know why Eh-reek's attentions should have this effect on me, especially as I'm not much enamored of his type, but my spirits soar as I think to myself *you don't have to go to the party, but boy, it's nice to be invited!*

The glow from the mountain air and the little flirtation must have brightened my eyes for when I open the door to the bedroom and trill a merry *'Bonsoir'*, Calm looks at me suspiciously over the book she's reading, places it face down in her lap, and says: 'OK. Who is it this time?'

It takes me a while to 'fess up to her about the possible rendezvous later this evening. I feel a bit guilty as I know she really fancies Hot Frog and I wouldn't want to upset her for the world. A Club Med *employé* is certainly not worth losing a friend for, no matter how delectable he is.

'Did you stop for a *vin chaud* on the way down?' I ask her casually, as I step out of the shower.

'Not tonight,' she answers. 'I was feeling a bit unsteady after that last run so I came straight back to the room.'

'It was horribly steep at the top,' I agree. 'I took a terrible tumble and ploughed home like a beginner. Then I got chatting to

Eh-reek . . . ' I stop mid-sentence not quite knowing how to tell her the rest.

'He's drop-dead gorgeous, isn't he?' she comments. 'You thinking of . . . ?'

'No, no!' I say hastily then I mumble, 'but he did ask if I fancied a drink after the show.'

CBF disappears into the wardrobe, hiding her reaction in the sound of hangers being dragged along a rail.

'White shirt with black jeans or red top with blue jeans?' she asks as she emerges holding various items against herself.

'Red with blue, definitely,' I say, relieved not to have been told off for once. I sit down at my makeshift dressing table and start drying my hair.

'So are you going?' she asks, as I switch off the dryer for a moment and twirl another section around the brush.

'I doubt it,' I answer pompously. 'Would you?'

'Course I would!' she says. 'And at least if you go I'll get to hear the gory details first hand.'

As we finish dressing for the evening, I take special care *not* to put on my best undies. Every woman knows that mismatched lingerie is an excellent deterrent.

Enjoying the secretive element of the impending assignation, I write my mobile number on a piece of paper and hide it up my sleeve. When I enter the dining room, I shake Hot Frog's hand as usual and slip the note between his fingers. He palms it like a well-practiced magician and winks imperceptibly with his dreamy green eyes. I smile and move on. Smooth as satin, sexy as silk.

Calm and I sit with HOM throughout dinner. He's as entertaining as ever, and I hardly notice CBF just picking at her food.

HOM and I head for the dessert buffet deep in conversation, but I stop halfway and wait for Calm to join us. She walks slowly towards me, one hand on her temple, the other on her tum. She's looking decidedly pale and shaky.

'You OK?' I ask anxiously.

'I'm not sure,' she says. 'I think I'll pass on dessert. I'm going to have an early night.'

'Do you want me to come back with you?' I offer, selfishly hoping she'll say no.

'I'll be fine,' she answers, then drops her voice to a whisper. 'I'll try and wait up for you. Have fun and be good!' and she walks off towards the lifts.

HOM and I finish our meal then repair to the bar where we order more drinks. I ask him about his life in London trying to ascertain if he's really single. He mentions a couple of short-lived affairs, nothing of any consequence. Strange at his age, I think to myself, but at least he's baggage-free, unlike me who has more baggage than British Airways.

Because I'm nervous about my impending date, I talk far too much, spilling out my excitement and trepidation at the imminent release of my book, *The Toyboy Diaries*. This is an autobiographical romp-a-thon through the past twenty years of my life, and I'm both elated and apprehensive about putting these private diaries in the public domain. The book describes my sexploits in great detail and features a procession of young men with whom I had the pleasure of sharing my sheets. It is an honest book that I'm proud to have written, but I know it is likely to shock a lot of people.

As he listens, he manages to smile and frown all at once which I find both confusing and endearing. I tell him my true age, which doesn't seem to faze him; in fact he immediately confesses to an irrepressible weakness for older women. For a moment we're both silent; perhaps, like me, he's thinking that a fifteen-year age gap is not such a big one, or perhaps he's contemplating my colourful past.

My gaze travels across his kindly face and soft brown eyes and I start to think of him not as a handsome *older* man but perhaps as The Right Man, or at least, the right sort of man for me. I recognize that I really like him, not in a superficial way but in a deeper, more considered manner. Tonight, however, the lure of adventure is too strong, and in any case, would I be able to cope with a Right Man? I only seem to get hooked on the Wrong Ones . . .

Just then he yawns, stretches and looks at his watch. It's 11.50 p.m.

'Past my bedtime,' he says and offers to walk me back to my room. I tell him I'll just sit here a little longer, enjoying the peace and quiet. The bar is almost empty, and as he leaves I sink back into my discreetly placed armchair to wait the midnight hour.

As I watch the staff clearing up, I remind myself that I am about to meet the man I vowed not to touch with a sterilized bargepole, which I have somehow failed to acquire and secrete about my person.

Never mind, it's only a drink, I say to myself, my selective memory blanking the fact that I had the same thought not so long ago and look where that got me . . .

I shrink down deeper into the armchair. I am on holiday, after all.

♀

At 11.56 p.m. Hot Frog texts to say he's free if I still want to meet, and if so, where am I? I text him back painstakingly one letter at a time. I'm too twitchy to reset my phone to French predictive. A few moments later, he appears at my side. He is wearing grey flannel trousers and a black cashmere polo shirt. God, he looks handsome, I think, thankful he's changed out of the gold pantaloons and scarlet cummerbund he wore when he hosted the cabaret earlier that evening.

'This isn't very appropriate,' I whisper, conscious of my reputation (huh?) and the odd G.O. still lurking around the bar.

He shrugs disarmingly, then whispers, 'Com and 'ave a dreenk in my rrroom.'

Having been unsure whether or not to even meet Hot Frog, now he is upon me, I cave immediately. He gives me directions to his quarters and slopes off with a satisfied smile. I follow at a discreet distance.

Hot Frog lives in a studio apartment at the top of the hotel. It looks like a heteropolitan's lair: dark walls, deep pile carpets, soft lighting, leather furniture. *Chilled Ibiza* grooves quietly in the corner. I'm pretty sure this place has seen a not inconsiderable amount of *sex*tra-curricular activity. I wonder if I'm about to become another notch on his bedpost (and he on mine).

The expected plying with alcohol prior to seduction does not take place. Instead, at my request, he pours me a fruit juice – I've drunk quite enough for one night – then opens a small bottle of water for himself. Sitting on separate sofas, we discuss his Club Med career and the rootlessness of a life spent six months here, two years there. He says he loves it, except when the customers complain. The loudest moaners apparently are his fellow citizens!

I enjoy chatting to him as I don't get much chance to practice my French. He compliments me again on my linguistic skills and I wonder whether I'm going to get a chance to find out about his. After a pleasant but fairly innocuous half hour, I finish my drink and look at my watch.

'Are you tired?' he asks immediately.

'Not particularly . . . '

'Zo why you want to go?' he says, and in one swift move he's kneeling before me and is applying his linguistic skills to the back of my throat.

I think how recently I was kneeling before MLP mourning the demise of our relationship. For a fleeting few seconds, I remember the meaningless distraction of Cute Face and Eurotrash, and then suddenly The Right Man appears in my head. I marvel at the serendipity of life and how quickly hearts can heal. Then I'm back in the moment in Val Dizzy Air, and everything else fades away . . .

Unfortunately I'm not sure I actually like being in *this* particular moment. Despite the fact that Hot Frog comes on like a galloping Gallic love machine, he has no idea how to kiss. He opens his mouth far too wide and his lingual swirling is wet and sloppy. This intended prelude to passion doesn't arouse me one little bit. I go along with it for a while then push him gently away and stand up.

He takes this as an invitation to lunge back in and kisses me again. But still I feel nothing. Not even close; definitely no cigar (apart from the *Upmann Gigante* growing in his trousers). I push him away again and this time he takes the rejection for

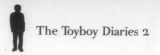

what it is, backing off like a gun victim with his hands held in the air. He wouldn't want to jeopardize his career by having a client cry 'rape' now, would he?

'Can you find your way back?' he asks.

'I think so,' I reply. 'I found my way here, didn't I?'

He takes hold of me again but I wriggle free and he opens the door to let me out.

'Come back if you get lost,' he calls as I wend my way towards the back stairs.

I return to the room feeling somewhat virtuous – a sensation I'm not overly familiar with – to find CBF still awake, as promised.

'Well?' she asks struggling to sit up in bed.

'Charming company and gilt-edged charisma,' I report.

'But . . . ?' she asks knowing there's a 'but' coming.

'He's a lousy kisser.'

She winces and shakes her head sympathetically.

'Can't have it all,' she says and slumps back on the pillow. We chat as I get undressed and eventually we fall asleep.

Nineteen

In the early hours of the morning, poor Calm Best Friend is propelled out of bed by a violent bout of vomiting which lasts the rest of the night and into the next day. There's not much I can do until morning, when I call a doctor and send a text to Hot Frog. As the manager, he needs to know the health status of his hotel guests.

He texts back to say he's sorry and asks if there's anything he can do. He also reminds me to wash my hands diligently if I'm caring for her.

He adds that he has a busy schedule that day, but would be free to see me again in the evening if I'd like. I think about this for the time it takes a mouse to blink and, because I'm a cussed, contrary cow, I decide that *oui*, I would like.

There's a whiteout brewing, so I forsake my skiing and stay in the room to look after Calm. She is shivery and feeling grim but I try to entertain her, reading articles from magazines and filling her in on the details from the night before. I stay until the doctor arrives then go down to the village to pick up the medicine that's been prescribed for her.

At lunchtime I pop into the dining room to get some consommé for the patient *et voilà!* Hot Frog is there as usual.

Despite his urgent need for snogging lessons, he still has sexuality oozing out of every pore. We share a secret smile and my attraction to him increases. If I could just train him to kiss properly, my holiday fantasies would be fulfilled.

Calm Best Friend is still feeling wretched but orders me to go down for dinner without her and enjoy my evening. This time, when I get dressed, I don my *just-in-case-I-get-lucky* undies. It would be a shame to waste them, wouldn't it?

I have no problem enjoying the company of two very different men at the same time, so am quite happy to spend the evening with The Right Man with whom I don't have to worry about the style of my lingerie. He is very easy to get on with. I feel I can talk to him about anything and am relaxed in his company, though I'm not altogether sure what he thinks about me. Later that evening we watch the cabaret show together and I lean up against him in the dark theatre imagining what a relief if would be to always feel this safe and this wonderful.

Just before midnight, he offers again to walk me to my room. Although I'm meeting Hot Frog later on, I want to look in on CBF and see that she's OK, so I accept. When the lift doors close and we're alone together, he reaches his hand up and strokes my hair, looking down at me with softness in his eyes. My heart hesitates for a moment as I smile up at him then resumes beating at a faster pace.

We walk along the corridor hand in hand. Feeling bemused at this sudden *rapprochment,* I can't quite believe that this lovely man is showing signs of interest in me. Could he really be The One? Could my rocky road finally become a tarmac-ed highway?

We stop outside my room and he leans down to kiss me. In confusion I turn my face away without, I hope, hurting his feelings. How can I possibly kiss *him* now and Monsieur le Grenouille Chaud later on? While these thoughts are rushing through my head, he leans towards me again and before I know it, I've sunk against the wall and we're locked together in a knee-trembling embrace. Now here's a chap who *really* knows how to kiss: tenderly yet with the promise of passion to come. I'm flustered when I realize he's really turned me on. How cruel and shameless of me to use him as my warm-up man, but he doesn't know this and what he doesn't know won't hurt him.

I pull away before we become overly engaged, but he begs a few minutes alone with me, which I find hard to refuse. I go into his room, mindful of the fact that the midnight text from Hot Frog is due through at any moment. Not having any pockets in my trousers, my mobile is wedged firmly between my breasts.

Sure enough, as The Right Man shuts his bedroom door and draws me close, I feel the vibration begin deep in my cleavage. I jump back from him suddenly, talking loudly to divert his attention.

'Gosh, your room's tidy for a bloke!' I shout, disturbing the romantic vibe between us. He looks rather puzzled as well he might. Knowing that my phone is set to repeat at one minute intervals, I dive back in for a quick clinch then pull away again just before my tits go off for a second time. This ridiculous hokey-cokey is hardly conducive to further romance and besides I have a date with someone else! Blushing and stammering with what I hope he takes to be girlish modesty, I peck him affectionately on both cheeks and reach for the door knob.

He stands there like a starving man who's happened across the only restaurant in town only to be told the kitchen's closed. I feel sorry and guilty, but tonight I am driven by unfinished business with a man who's had more women than Winner's had dinners and for some unknown reason, he is my choice *du soir*.

I hare off to my room to check on CBF. She's sleeping peacefully so I touch up my make-up then dash out the door, dive into the stairwell and leg it up to the fourth floor. Hot Frog's door is ajar and I slide in quietly. He's sitting on his sofa deliciously decked out in a black open-necked shirt and gabardine trousers like a panther coolly awaiting his prey. He rises to greet me, pours me a fruit juice and we chat about the day, then all at once he's in my face again with his big, wet kiss. Do I dare tell a Frenchman how to perform this basic act? Needs must.

'Can I show how I *really love* to be kissed?' I breathe seductively, and not waiting for an answer, I close his lips with my thumb and forefinger.

'*Ferme ta bouche*,' I command, 'and do as I do.'

I lick my lips and brush them lightly against his. Emitting a low moan, he mirrors my motion. Our moist mouths slide sensuously across each other's, our tongues licking, flicking, in a less-is-more kind of way. If I achieve nothing else on this holiday, at least I'll have sent this amateur on his way with one proficient skill.

He unbuttons his shirt and guides my hand over his chest to his erect nipple. I rub it lightly and he groans and presses the length of his body against mine. His hand is flat on my *derrière*, pushing me against him as his increasing hardness fills the space between us. I grind into him and he breathes in sharply and whips me around. With his hands on my hips and his pistol in the small of my back, he walks me towards the sofa where I collapse in an abandoned heap.

He stretches out alongside me and yanks up my top, fondling my breast in his hand while he dips his head to gorge on my nipple. The sensation shoots straight to my nerve centre and I gasp and shudder.

He flips open the button at my waistband, pulls down my zip and dives his hand inside my trousers, prising aside my panties to find my moist and creamy wetness. I pulsate immediately against his rubbing finger and we rip the rest of our clothes off and writhe naked on the leather sofa.

He stands up abruptly, his profile making a perfect hoop-la, and pulls me to my feet. Then he pushes me towards the bedroom and we sink down on his big white bed.

'I want to kiss you everywhere,' he pants into my mouth.

'Well no one's stopping you . . . ' I pant back and he tongues his way down my body until he reaches my parted thighs and dives in to devour me hungrily. I push and buck against him until I come again and cry out joyously at that special compliment MLP would never pay me.

Hot Frog eats me avidly until I beg him to stop – the sensation is now too sharp and sensitive. He climbs up and straddles my chest, his eager cock bobbing inches from my face. I stick my tongue out and lick the tip. He moves it forward against my lips and I suckle on it gently. He reaches over to his bedside table, rips open a condom, puts it on, slides back down me and plunges in. He grinds a few times, stiffens, cries out and comes.

As he relaxes, he wraps me warmly in his arms. 'Chéri, zat was wunder-fool,' he murmurs.

I'm surprised at the affection he's showing me. I had him down as a *Wham Bam Mon Dieu Is That The Time?* man. He hugs and strokes me lovingly until I say it's time to go, then we both get dressed and he sees me politely to the door. We kiss goodnight and I sneak back through the quiet corridors to the safety of the room.

CBF stirs but doesn't wake. With a pang of remorse, I think of The Right Man sleeping soundly down the hall. If he knew what a slag he'd set his sights on, I'm sure he'd chuck me, right here, right now.

The next day is spent skiing in the morning and playing Scrabble with some of the other guests in the afternoon. Calm, poor thing, is still unwell, and after taking her some pasta for lunch, which she picks at then pushes away, I leave her to sleep in peace.

Later that afternoon I receive two texts. The first is from Hot Frog to say how much he enjoyed last night and would I be free to meet again on Saturday after the show? I am very surprised at this; I'd have thought he'd be doing 'customer liaison' with someone else by now. Saturday will be the last night of the holiday but I'm not sure whether a repeat performance is really what I want or need from him.

The second text takes me even more by surprise and I have to read it twice before I realize who it's from. *Some afternoon time alone with you is tempting me off the mountain early. I am battling through a blizzard towards you. 5 mins together would be so perfect. x*

I don't recognize the number but I can only assume it's from The Right Man. Instantly I'm thrown into confusion. I hurry back to the room to discuss my dilemma with Calm Best Friend. The pasta is where I left it, cold and congealed and looking unappetizing. I put the plate outside the door to return it to the dining room, then sit down on the side of the bed and

peer at my poor dear friend. She opens one eye, attempts the faintest of smiles, shudders nauseously and shuts it again.

I'm desperate to talk to her. CBF's advice is invariably helpful in these crisis situations, even if I don't always take it. However I decide it's not fair to inflict my fickle fidelity on her when she's so weak and feeble. I run a flannel under the cold water and lay it across her forehead. She smiles gratefully but there's not a lot else she can do. I sit with her for half an hour, make sure she's comfortable and taking in fluids and watch her fall back to sleep. Then I creep to the door, let myself out and head for the bar.

I haven't made my mind up what to do about The Right Man yet. I'd really rather wait until we're back in London – I feel he's too important to treat like just another holiday romance. I sit absently by the window, looking at the whirling snow outside and wondering what to say in response to his text. And as I dither and ponder, fate makes the decision for me. For there he is, freshly showered and looking divine. He brushes my body with the soupçon of a smile and heads back invitingly towards the lifts. Like a sleepwalker, I get up, mumble an excuse to anyone who is listening, leave the bar and follow him.

Exhilaration, anticipation, self-loathing and reproach mingle inside me like uninvited guests at a sinister cocktail party. Why does doing wrong somehow feel so right? As the lift door closes on us, I think about what's happening. Maybe this screwy ski trip is part of some pre-ordained Feast Cycle, in which case I'd better embrace it for all its worth, for when the famine returns – which it will – I'll only have the memories to feed on.

The Right Man and I look at each other fondly. Then we hurry to his room like furtive teenagers. He hangs the *Do Not Disturb* sign on the door and shuts it quietly behind us. As I pass the bathroom, I notice a whole pharmacy of medication laid out on the shelves. I feel awkward to have spotted this, like I've intruded on his privacy. I wonder what is wrong with him to need so many pills, but the thought, like all others, is banished as he draws me tenderly to him.

We sink down onto the bed and an unfamiliar sensation wafts over me, like a warm wind over a lonely moor. I feel so very peaceful with this man, so shielded. With no words spoken, we lie down together and he plants a thousand kisses on my face and neck. The atmosphere in the room assumes a dream-like quality. The outside world is still and silent, disappearing beneath a blanket of freshly fallen snow.

'I've longed to be held like this,' I whisper, 'by someone who cares enough not to need anything more.'

He gathers me closer to him and murmurs in my hair, 'I can do that.'

A shudder of emotion travels through me releasing so much pressure it makes me want to weep. I crush my head against his chest and he rocks me like a baby. I wish that we could stay like this forever.

The afternoon drifts gently by. He calms me with his kisses and our slow and subtle exploration of each other inevitably becomes more sexually charged. With no need for question or answer, we undress; a primal urge now drives us – we must be skin to skin. The lightness of his touch is like the breath of angels. He takes me to a place so blissful and serene, I seem to float above myself. And when he finally enters me, we do not have sex. We make love.

Later that night, having dined with the confidence of a couple who share a special secret, we slip away to his room and make love once again. Much later, as I lie in bed listening to his quiet breathing, I am strangely touched by how comfortable I feel with this man. And yet, for no apparent reason, I feel something's not quite right. He has a quiet control about him, as though he's withholding something he dare not release. I can't quite put my finger on it, but my instinct says 'be careful'.

The next day is the last of the holiday and I am determined to spend it with Calm Best Friend. Happily, she is up and about but still feeling fragile. Instead of skiing, we go for a long walk and window-shop our way through the town. By late afternoon, some of the colour has returned to her cheeks. We have a quiet supper together and then go up to our room to pack. As I pass The Right Man in the dining room we smile intimately at each other. I'm hoping to see him again back in London. He's agreed to come home with me after we land, averting the need for any awkward Gatwick goodbyes. I'm quietly confident that we have a future, but I've learned not to trust *faits* until they're *accomplis*.

Calm hefts her suitcase out from under the bed then looks gloomily at the piles of clothes she has to pack.

'I bought so many new things for this trip and I've hardly worn any of them,' she moans as she folds her garments carefully and lays them in the case.

'I'm sure their time will come,' I assure her as I do the same with mine.

'Bloody food poisoning stole my holiday,' she goes on. 'Shame you can't claim for Loss of No-Strings Sex on the insurance!'

I'm about to say 'I had enough for both of us' but manage to restrain myself.

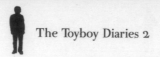

'You're looking awfully skinny though,' I say trying to appease her. 'That's got to be worth more than "no-strings sex" any day!'

She nods in agreement and we both laugh.

'I can't thank you enough for suggesting this trip,' I tell her later as we sit together in the bar, sipping medicinal brandy and gazing at the dark, looming mountains and bright stars outside.

She looks at me attentively with her head cocked on one side. 'You do look different,' she agrees. 'Renewed, somehow.'

I pause, wondering whether to share my feelings about The Right Man. 'Something significant has happened,' I say carefully. 'I think I've met someone I could actually stay with for a very long time. And more importantly, I really want to!'

Weakened as she is by her bout of sickness, she simply nods and puts an affectionate hand on mine. We turn in soon after, knowing we've a long journey ahead. Unbeknown to me, my journey turns out to be a lot longer than hers.

Twenty

I arrive home with The Right Man around 3 p.m. We dump our bags, shower quickly and go straight to bed. This is a first for me – I usually phone the family then unpack and put a wash on – but the circumstances today are exceptional. I can't quite believe I've got him in my home like this: it feels so natural, as if he was always meant to be here. We make love slowly, with purity and respect, comfortable in our growing knowledge of each other and with a surprising depth of intimacy for two people who only met a week ago. Then we lay together dozing until it gets dark.

After a while, I get up to forage for food. We didn't even stop for milk on the way back from the airport, but I have the oozy Reblochon cheese I bought in the resort and bread, as always, in the freezer. I pop a baguette in the oven and bring the snack back to bed on a tray with a bottle of wine. TRM seems delighted at this impromptu picnic, which we devour together like a couple of kids at a midnight feast.

I imagine this is how we will spend many future times and I sigh with pleasure and relief that my years of single struggle may soon be over. And how proud I will be of us as a couple! Some-one I can introduce at last to my family and friends without them curling their toes up in embarrassment. Unashamedly, I rush ahead of myself with talk of long weekends away and holidays, mapping out our future like a stairway to the stars. I tell him I would love to have someone to look after, a partner to shop and cook for, a man's shirts in my washing-machine again.

He absorbs this information without interrupting me and, lulled into a false sense of security by what I imagine to be his willing acceptance of everything I say, I carry on talking. I tell him more about my convoluted past: my two difficult marriages, two worse divorces, one seven-year relationship with a man twenty-one years my junior, a catalogue of short-lived affairs leading nowhere . . . and I crown it all by saying how thrilled I am that my troubled times may soon be over now that he – The Right Man – has arrived in my life. I hardly notice that he grows quieter and quieter the more I talk. Eventually we fall asleep, curled up in each other's arms.

Two of the craziest weeks of my life follow. My book, *The Toyboy Diaries*, is launched and I'm caught up in a flurry of publicity that I cannot stop. Like Diana's sister said to her the night before the Royal Wedding: 'You can't back out now, Duch, your face is on the tea towels.'

Although I am proud of my literary achievement, I'm slightly worried about the subject matter and the timing. I hope all this exposure will not have any adverse affect on TRM and his feelings for me. My feelings for him are growing with each passing day, as I fantasize about the life we'll have together as soon as my hectic schedule settles down. Rushing from radio interview to TV appearance, I keep the flame alive on simmer as I embrace my fifteen minutes of fame for all it's worth.

Although my daughters have a grudging admiration that their mother is on *This Morning* and *Richard & Judy*, I've banned them from reading the book. Children don't want to know about their parents' sex lives even if the parents are married to each other. Mine certainly don't want their regard for me marred by vivid descriptions of me lying on my back (front and sides!) with my legs in the air. They cannot, however, miss the stories that are splashed across the newspapers. I feign bravado and laugh it off, but I'm slightly uncomfortable that judgmental journalists are chewing over my life choices, some with fascination and some with horror.

My mother sniffs and purses her lips, uncertain of whether to feel pride or indignation. Poppy mumbles something about 'washing your dirty laundry in the village well,' and Lily changes the subject every time I dare to broach it. My sister compliments me hesitantly on my success, but she too is slightly disconcerted about what people might think. But there are many voices of approbation to counter these attacks, compliments and thanks from other women who claim I've 'changed the way they look at life.' A flattering flutter of fan mail arrives daily in my email inbox.

So caught up am I in the maelstrom of the moment, I haven't had time to arrange another get-together with TRM. I haven't actually heard much from him since he left my bed on our return from holiday. A text here, a voicemail message there, both, I note, in one direction: from me to him. I try not to obsess too much and I continue on the publicity bandwagon, talking fluent *toyboy* while thinking somewhat deceitfully that my days of dalliances with this much-loved species may soon be over.

One evening, when things have begun to settle down, I do manage to get through to TRM on the phone. The conversation is a little stilted at first – we seem to have lost the momentum that had been building up between us. I tell him I'd love to see him again, suggest we meet up as soon as is convenient, but we can't seem to fix a date that suits us both. At the back of my mind I'm worried that he's read some dubious publicity and has decided that I'm not the girl for him. He never mentions anything though so I keep quiet, secretly hoping that it's all passed him by.

As soon as the pressure has died down, I tell myself, I'll be able to give my full attention to this relationship and turn it into something durable and worthwhile. I haven't forgotten how wonderful he made me feel and I'm still convinced that he and I have a future.

During a rushed lunch with Newly Single one day, she remarks that I'm talking like a steam train and eating like a horse.

'If you were any younger,' she comments, 'I'd say you might be pregnant! You're certainly glowing. You changed your make-up or something?'

'Changed my life more like!' I reply. 'And thank God for HRT! Plus I've upped my vitamin intake to help me through this busy time. I need to stay fit for TRM, he's not quite 47 you know. Old enough by society's standards yet young enough for me!'

'So when did you last see him?' she asks which stops me in my tracks.

'Not since we got back from holiday,' I answer pensively, slowing my spoon midway between tiramisu and mouth.

'Not exactly chomping at the bit, is he?' she comments, giving me a discomfiting *think-about-it* gaze.

'Well I've hardly had time, have I?' I say defensively. 'And as for behaving like I might be pregnant, I'd love to have his children, if there was still womb at the inn!'

'You do know the risks involved in prolonged use of HRT?' she asks, suddenly going into medical mode.

'Of course I do,' I answer, and carry on eating.

In fact, this is an issue I'm often asked about. Following a hysterectomy at the age of 45, I was put on HRT to which I have an unswerving devotion. My gynecologist says I can stay on it until my dying day and if I'm honest, I fear giving it up lest I awake one morning with a tight grey perm and loose grey skin. And as for the middle-aged dress code, I'm with Amy Winehouse on that one:

They tried to make me go to Windsmoor, I said No, No, NO!

It's not just about appearance though. I'm aware of the negatives associated with hormone replacement   most notably an increased risk of breast cancer – but the positives are also too numerous to ignore. My mother suffers from heart disease and osteoporosis and ladies who have opted not to – or for health reasons cannot – use HRT, have less energy and *joie de vivre* and, more importantly, a lot less libido.

Some may say: 'Thank God for that' and take up bowls or gardening. Others run the risk of being diagnosed with – I can't even bear to say it – atrophied vagina. This is when poor old puss has been so starved of oestrogen that she shrivels up and dies. For this very reason, we need to include sex in our diets and if we can't find anyone to do it with, there are plenty of toys on the market to do it for us. Learning to love yourself *is* the greatest love of all.

♀

With another week drawing to a close, I become increasingly anxious by the inability of The Right Man and I to fix a date. It irks me that *he* hasn't made any effort to get in touch but I tell myself he's probably busy and he knows I am too. I hate to make all the running, especially with someone as important to me as him, but one evening when I'm home alone, I decide to instigate a little charm offensive and so I dial his number.

My heartbeat speeds up as I wait for him to answer. Then suddenly there he is, sounding cheerful and reasonably pleased to hear from me. My spirits rise as I listen to him talk; his lilting voice is warm and mellifluous. Despite it being 8.23 p.m. he tells me he's 'still in the office being boring'.

We talk about what we've both been up to: I've been studying the Sacrament of Holy Orders obviously, and he says he's been mostly working late. When the conversation looks like it's about to run out of gas, I leap into the driving seat and slam my foot on the accelerator.

'I was thinking of making a fondue one night,' I say, winging it as I am wont to do. 'It would be pointless my making it just for one so I wondered' – I hold my breath and pray to all the Gods and Saints – 'would you like to come over and fondue with me?'

I'm half-expecting a hesitation or a refusal and am thrilled beyond belief when he answers, 'Sounds like a nice idea but I really should take you out.'

I manage not to shout 'Yes! Yes!' like Meg Ryan in *When Harry Met Sally* and I take a deep breath and answer casually. 'Well, either way is fine by me . . . but why don't I do the fondue this time and then you can take me out the time after that.' And just in case he's about to say *I'll check my diary and call you sometime* I steam on with, 'How about next Thursday?'

He can't do Thursday, I can't do Wednesday so we make a date for twelve days hence. That's Twelve Days . . .

Hence.

'Half seven?' he asks, precise enough to firm up the arrangement.

'Perfect!' I reply and we say our goodbyes.

I walk over to the hall mirror and kiss myself full on the mouth. I punch the air, dance the funky chicken and moonwalk backwards down the corridor until I reach my bedroom.

Did you see what I just did there? I ask the curtains.

I made something happen.

Yes, I did.

OH YES I DID!

In an effort to make the twelve days hence pass faster, I invite a mixed bag of older single friends over one evening to discuss forming a theatre group. That's as in *going to*, not *acting in* – although right now I feel like I could star in any Victorian melodrama you'd care to throw at me. I have my own Heathcliff waiting in the wings . . . though at this point I still think of him as Mr. Darcy.

'So what's happening in *your* love life?' Half Empty asks gloomily as she follows me into the kitchen.

'I'm, er, I'm seeing that chap I met on holiday soon,' I answer casually, not wishing to boast to someone who has no one at present.

'Sounds like you've got yourself sorted then,' she sniffs somewhat grudgingly. 'So you won't need this singles group after all. Unlike me . . . '

'Well nothing's set in stone,' I answer, while my inner stonemason hammers TRM's name and mine into a slab of rock surrounded by a heart.

Over a spread of sandwiches and pastries, the buddies and I research all of London's fringe venues and compile a list of plays, musicals and master classes we'd like to attend. Everyone volunteers to bring a friend, someone the others may not know. I move around the table pouring teas and coffees while Newly Single jots down names on the membership list.

'What about Raymond?' suggests one of our male friends.

'Not Raymond with the grey shoes?' I ask.

'Oh, the one you always call *Graymond*?' blurts Half Empty tactfully.

I hear a sniggering from the end of the table where CBF is sitting with Blondie. Half Empty opens her mouth to say something else but stops in mid-track as I shake my head furiously. There are other men present – good friends of mine all – some of whom have also slipped past the Wardrobe Police. Now is not the time to comment further on Graymond's style bypass in the shoe department. Newly Single adds him to the list and we arrange the first outing for the following week.

I spend a lot of time 'looking forward' as the 'twelve days hence' pass slowly by. This is the most tremendous form of foreplay. I agonize about how I should be when The Right Man arrives: how to act, what to say, what to wear. Should I be light and fluffy? Sexy and seductive? Deep and serious? Should I greet him at the door in fishnet stockings and black suspenders? A modest grey dress with a Peter Pan collar? A nun's habit? A bridal gown?

I vacillate over whether to wait for him at the front door, or leave it open and be in the kitchen when he walks in. Perhaps I'll drop to my knees as he enters and beg him to forgive me my transgressions. While I'm down there I might as well give him a blow job.

Time drags by like a half-dead donkey. Every time the phone rings I leap like a salmon, convinced it's him calling to cancel. I get invited to a fairly important business drinks party on the same evening as our date. Changing our arrangement or asking him to come over later is unthinkable. The arrangement is as fragile as the last leaf of autumn: the slightest breeze could take it down.

A few days before the projected rendezvous, I dare myself to buy the cheese for the fondue. I plan the rest of the menu meticulously, like Gordon, Jamie, Delia and Heston are all coming to dinner.

Finally the longed-for day arrives and with it, The Right Man. As (bad) luck would have it, there was an article about me in the papers that morning but I'm sure this erudite male doesn't read the tabloids. But as I trip happily to the door to greet him in my carefully selected, lady-with-hidden-vamp outfit, I know at once that something is terribly wrong.

'If you like *toyboys* so much,' he says, spitting out the word like venom almost before he crosses the threshold, 'why on earth are you interested in me? I'm 47, for God's sake. Practically geriatric!'

Oh Shit! Oh Bugger! Oh fuck! Fuck! FUCK! He must have seen today's *Daily Mail*.

'You're not!' I argue desperately. 'You're perfect. And I'm done with all that . . . '

He stomps into my living room and sits down. 'Not according to the press, you're not!'

'Why don't I give you a copy of the book?' I suggest stupidly, trying to placate him. 'It's nowhere near as bad as you think, especially as most of it is made up . . . ' and without thinking, I pluck a newly minted copy from my shelf and drop it in his lap.

And then I realize what I've done. I've shot myself, not only in the foot, but in the head and heart as well. There's a reference to sex every four pages. That's *me* having sex – every four pages!

'Please don't throw things at me,' he bleats reproachfully, looking at his lap like I've just poured green slime all over it. 'And please don't shout.'

At this point I really should have given up. If we do ever actually get together, I think, I'd have to temper my entire personality to suit his sensibilities. Instead I apologize and reach out to take the book from him.

He snatches it back and turns it over suspiciously, as if it could potentially go off in his hand. Scowling with revulsion, he reads the back cover. I stand there chewing my thumb, feeling like a schoolgirl whose father's just received a letter from the head informing him that she's been caught sniffing coke off the gym teacher's cock.

'How can it possibly work between us?' he shrieks a moment later, having scanned the synopsis. 'You'll always be looking over my shoulder for the next 19-year-old!'

'I will not!' I cry defensively. 'That affair happened twenty years ago and I'm *so* over it now . . . '

I trail off. My teeth ache at the denials being pushed through them. But it doesn't matter anyway. For whatever I say or do, the thing I dreaded most is happening: it's all beginning to fall apart.

Over the next few hours this tall, upright, confident, accomplished, funny, genial man shrivels like a burst balloon. In his place appears an ailing, timid, frightened, suspicious wreck. I don't recognize him at all.

He talks about past relationships that haven't worked out, deep insecurities he's always suffered from, low self-esteem, a plethora of illnesses (hence all the pills) and an overwhelming conviction that, like all the males in his family, he too will die young.

'And you've had such a full and varied life,' he bemoans accusingly. 'How could I keep up? And I *cannot* allow myself to fall in love with you. I'm just not strong enough. I would get terribly hurt. And . . . ' he drops his voice to a whisper, 'I cannot have sex without love . . .'

Oh can't you? I think indignantly. *You managed it well enough not so long ago.*

I absorb what he tells me with a mixture of resentment and disbelief. I'm prepared to make a huge emotional investment but he is running scared. He says he's not strong enough to be with a woman like me, but I think he is *very* strong, very strong indeed to make such an unwavering decision. After all, if love were a choice, would any of us choose such dark, exquisite torment?

As I listen to his fears and his distrust, I regret each and every occasion I spoke to him honestly and freely, both on holiday and on the night we came home. I suppose, that first evening we sat talking together in France, I may have crowed about my conquests, past and present. I didn't realize then that I would fall for him. The very honesty of our conversations *made* me fall for him – how ironic that it should now come back to haunt me!

He probably suspects my inability to be faithful and he's right, of course. I remember Hot Frog with a pang, and recall how I joked to The Right Man at one point that as a girlfriend I was probably 'a very bad bet'. I was daring him even then to love me, but he does not dare. He does not dare at all.

Over the next hour I try to reinvent myself. I tell him that my past is in the past, that I'm ready for a new beginning, that

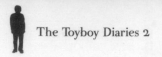

I'd love my future to be spent with him, but he is resolutely unconvinced. I feel suddenly confused by my role; I sound like an alpha male trying to seduce a reluctant virgin.

Eventually, unable to bear the stress of my insistence any longer, my *not quite* Right Man breaks down and sobs in my arms. I comfort him as best I can, but I know now that the warning instinct that told me 'be careful' was right. This man cannot sustain a relationship with me; he cannot even sustain one with himself.

At midnight, with no further distance for us to travel, he gets up and leaves. I'm now the weaker and he's the stronger. He hugs me briefly at the door and descends dejected down the stairs.

He's just a man, I tell myself as I stand by the window and watch him walk away. And if I charmed him once, surely I can charm him again?

An acerbic little motto comes to mind and a spark of optimism flares inside me. *You can't make somebody love you. All you can do is stalk them and hope that one day they'll give in.*

I stay by the window for a very long time, thinking about what to do next and watching the moon rise slowly in the night sky. It's only when I stir myself and head for bed that I realize he's taken the book with him.

The next morning I text him: *My dearest darling, I'm shattered by what happened last night. I'm really going to miss you xxx*

A day passes before his reply. *I'm really sorry lovely Wendy but this overly private and sensitive man cannot do this. I wish I could but I can't. Sorry sorry sorry. Xx*

Twenty-One

My mother, with whom I didn't always have the best relationship, once said, 'Wendy could fall in a dustbin and come out smelling of roses.' At the moment though, all I'm sniffing is the sour scent of loss.

I'm offering TRM the best of my love and he doesn't bloody want it! He's a coward. He doesn't want to play. If you don't play, you can't lose.

Despite this, something in my genetic make-up will not allow me to accept defeat. A long line of oppressed ancestors battled their way out of Russia, Latvia and Lithuania and dispersed to the four corners of the globe. They not only survived, they made a go of it. Taught their stories from a young age, I was conditioned to strive for success and this philosophy has encouraged me on my journey ever since. I don't compare my experiences to theirs, of course; but at the same time I have learned that some things must be fought for – if you chase your dreams hard enough, one day you'll catch them.

The trouble is I kind of understand where TRM is coming from: his fear of falling in love then having his heart ripped out is a very valid one. I'm also aware that I'm in danger of getting far too carried away with this less than magnificent obsession. I seem to have projected all my needs onto him based on very little, but I'm not prepared to let him go without a fight.

The following Tuesday is the first singles group theatre outing: an obscure play by an unknown writer at a small fringe theatre in Dalston. Among the crowd that turns out is Graymond. He makes a beeline for the empty seat next to me, plonks himself down and starts babbling. I'm tired and have a slight headache and his voice is far too grating. As the lights dim and the curtain rises, I'm irritated that he's still talking so I tap him on the arm to shush him. Moments later, when he absentmindedly rustles his sweet packet, I smack his hand reproachfully and take the sweets away. He pulls a sulky face and looks at me sheepishly. Men are such babies, but in fairness I know I'm taking my disappointment out on him and everyone else.

After the performance, a dreary and doom-laded piece I can't remember much about, we go for a meal. Graymond sits opposite me, talking at, rather than to, one of the other women. He's giving her a précis of the play she's just seen as if she hadn't been there and I have no option but to listen. I realize that despite myself, I find him interesting; his take on it is alternative and shrewd and I study him as he's pontificating.

He's not bad looking for a 64-year-old: good strong features not yet blurred around the edges, salt and pepper hair, funky little glasses and a lopsided grin.

The Right Man had a lopsided grin too. I wonder if I'll ever see it again.

When I finally arrive home, tired and disgruntled, I suddenly decide I'm going to phone him. I psych myself up for at least an hour, feet pacing, heart racing, my mind composing disjointed phrases which fly around in my head like some windblown alphabet I can't make any sense of. Finally, with a dry throat and a speeding pulse, I dial his number. It rings a few times and goes to voicemail.

'Hello?' I say hesitantly. 'It's . . . er . . . Wendy . . . I'm not sure if I'm allowed to do this? Ring you, I mean. As a friend or whatever I may be,' and I break into a nervous laugh. 'I just wanted to say . . . I think about you all the time and I'd really like to know how you are? You see, I . . . er . . . I really miss you? And I care about you? And, er . . . it would be nice to hear from you?'

I have no idea why I'm talking with this querying Australian twang but as I replace the handset on the charger I know I sounded vulnerable and insecure. Despite this I feel marginally happier. What I've created by making this call is renewed hope – hope that he will call me back. Had there been a brick wall within bashing distance, I may as well have banged my head against it; but hope springs eternal, and that is my device.

Six days pass and I hear nothing from The Right Man. I work on my book on future collectibles and have lunch at Le Caprice with the pretty young editor of *Condé Nast Traveller*. I'm hoping to sell them some travel articles. I drink a very large, very pink Cosmopolitan and indulge in two hours of girlie chat with some business thrown in.

Later on another woman joins us: attractive, around 50, newly divorced, top-to-toe Chanel, face lift. She orders a bottle of champagne and we move on to the subject of my social situation. After listening to the story of The Right Man, the tipsy women are soon hard at work analyzing the ins and outs. Unfortunately there are rather more 'outs' than 'ins'. Face Lift suggests that I should ask him, in the most wounded voice that I can muster, whether the holiday romance was just a bit of fun for him, and explain that it was deadly serious for me. *Make him feel guilty*, she advises, *for having led you on.*

I nod agreeably but I know that isn't true. It was I who led myself on. I smile at her to thank her but she doesn't smile back. The face lift is very recent.

The following weekend I receive opposing advice. During a two-mile power walk through Kenwood with Calm Best Friend, I again address my dilemma about The Right Man. She's the only one I can talk to who really understands me as she actually met him and saw him at his sparkling best.

'I don't know where to go with this now,' I pant as we march along in tandem. 'Is there . . . *phew!* . . . *this is steep* . . . anything else I can reasonably do?'

Calm strides along beside me not saying very much. I know she's mulling it over and will give me the best advice possible whether I choose to take it or not.

'It's important . . . ' she says breathlessly, as we reach the top of the hill, 'to stay cool. Less is always more.'

'Oh I know,' I say, avoiding one puddle only to splosh into the next. 'But at the moment less equals zero. I'm trying to be bright and breezy but I'm about three steps away from a shot gun.'

'Are you sure he's worth it?' she asks as we head down the vale towards the café.

'*Uhnn* . . . ' I groan, 'Who knows? I thought so, but now . . .' I pause in the long grass to scrape the mud off my trainers, 'he's about as much use to me as a . . . as a glacier mint to a polar bear.'

Although it is CBF's nature to be kind and supportive, she's skeptical about it working out. She gently advises me not to invest more than I'm prepared to lose. I take note but not necessarily heed.

By the following Wednesday I still haven't heard from him so I decide to adopt a reverse philosophy: if he doesn't call today, I shall be relieved. I shall pray it's not him every time the phone rings, and be thankful when it isn't. In the spirit of this new approach I spend time glaring at my mobile muttering, 'Don't you dare ring, you bastard! Stay away from me!'

It seems to be doing the trick. That and the Bach Flower Remedy that Lily has prepared for me. She's a nutritional therapist and homeopathic consultant with the diploma to prove it. In her professional capacity she gave me a consultation, and before I knew it I found myself talking to her like she was my personal shrink. I told her about my emotional struggle; maybe as her mother I shouldn't have, but she took it in her stride. She's a good kid, our Lil.

She wrote it all down then went off to prepare a potion. She added wild hawthorn for anxiety, walnut for melancholy, marjoram root for self-determination and arsenic in case none of the above worked. I took eight drops straight away and immediately started feeling better.

My cure is aided and abetted by the arrival of my grand daughters, who are dropped off by a more than usually stressed-out Poppy to spend the night with me. She looks like she could do with a break and I'm happy for the distraction. Dealing with Tamara and Melodie however is like trying to tame a pair of electric eels. They are wriggly, demanding and hyperactive, and I have to call them ten times to come to the table for supper as they're busy setting up a jewellery shop to sell all my beads and baubles back to me. Once I've fed them, read to them and sent them to bed, then read to them again and sent them to bed several more times, I am shattered but also feel much more clear-headed and somehow calmer. I look at my mobile phone sitting serenely on the kitchen table. Not a peep from it all night.

'So glad you took the hint!' I say, feigning exultancy, but I don't believe it for a minute. Then I pick it up, switch it off and collapse, exhausted, into bed.

The next day, having returned my adorable little girlies to their rightful owners and mopped up the inevitable mess from all over my flat, I decide it's time to pay Eurotrash a return visit at his gallery. I need to give his art book back – and at the same time, I can't help wondering if something else might come of it. I'm tired of waiting round for The Right Man to call – it's been weeks now – and as a red-blooded woman, I need a bit of male attention to keep me and my corpuscles happy.

I catch Eurotrash on the hop, hungover, dishevelled and looking grungy. He's short-staffed, sweating and puffing as he drags some really naff pieces of 1970s gear around the gallery, rearranging the room settings. The minute he sets eyes on me, he begins waving his arms in the air like a drowning child, running his fingers through his hair, stroking his unshaven chin and pulling at his shirt. He's plainly not expecting lady callers. Enjoying his discomfiture, I approach to greet him. He covers his mouth with his hand.

'*Mein Gott!*' he exclaims. 'Vy you didn't tell me you voz coming? I'ff chust eaten a Libanese! I must shtink!'

I sniff the air around him and wrinkle up my nose.

'Com see ze new additions!' he cries excitedly and grabs my hand, proudly pointing out the sort of furniture impoverished newly-weds from my generation used to buy only to throw out the minute they could afford something better.

Once we are at the far end of the showroom, he abruptly puts his sartorial and halitosis-related unease aside and lunges forward to kiss me. It's like licking the bottom of an unwashed pot in the kitchen of a Beirut brothel. I lurch backwards and push him away.

'Look vot you do to me!' he declares engagingly, adjusting his erection this way and that. I cannot help but drop my eyes to the bulge in his trousers, which looks like the knob of a Zulu fighting stick.

He flattens me against the wall and tells me how much he's missed me and what a high he's been on since our last date, weeks ago. I turn my head away but am quite taken aback by this declaration.

'So why didn't you call me?' I ask.

'You told me you voz zeeing zomevun,' he shrugs, 'zo I'd take a shtep beck und vait.'

Fair point. Although my Plaster Master Disaster is long over, I haven't had the chance to tell Eurotrash that I seem to be single once again. And once again.

'Well things aren't too great to be honest . . . ' I confide, delaying the break-up retrospectively. The Hanoverian's eyes flash a mixture of interest and panic, and I take pity on him.

'But I'm sure we'll work it out,' I decide, not knowing who – or what – I'm talking about. Either way, I'm pretty certain I don't want to get involved with this shady character. I don't trust him one little bit: he smacks of decadence in a 'Berlin 1933' sort of way. And so, with a friendly peck on the cheek, I bid him good-bye and head out of his gallery feeling like a lioness abandoning the remains of her prey.

That evening the girls and I get together for our monthly summit. We're at Gilgamesh in Camden Town drinking Screaming Orgasms and digging into their mouth-watering Duck, Watermelon and Cashew Nut salad. One by one, we fill each other in on the gossip.

Blondie's bought a puppy so she can have 'unconditional love from someone who won't fuck with her head.' Calm is seeing a new man she met at a brainstorming meeting and it's developing rather well. Sensible is happily ensconced in her long-term relationship. Even Half Empty's dating, so until further notice, she's to be referred to as Half Full.

And then there's me.

'What news of your holiday romance?' asks Sensible. 'Have you heard from him recently?'

'Well I don't know if he's rung you, but he certainly hasn't rung me,' I answer miserably. 'I've done what I can to forget him. Old reliables, new maybes, work, family, verbally abusing my mobile phone, Bach flower remedies . . . I still think about him *all* the time.'

'Well, make another move. What are you waiting for? He'll get snapped up if you're not careful! That's right!'

'I don't think he wants to be snapped,' I reply.

'What about slapped?' asks Blondie in her inimitable dead-pan fashion.

'Some men need a bit of encouragement,' comments Calm

changing her tack from our previous discussion. A fresh round of cocktails arrives and by the time we've drunk them, they've convinced me to give him another shot.

When I return home that evening, I toy with my mobile wondering if I'm feeling strong and stupid enough to text The Right Man. I know it's a dead-end street but something drives me on. I decide to leave it for one more day and sit down in front of the computer.

Time for a distraction, I think, as I log on to toyboywarehouse.com. There have been a whole host of new sign-ups in the last couple of months, and a stack of winks and messages waiting for me. I scroll through them and find myself making a half-hearted date for Friday with a Brad Pitt look-a-like. I need something to look forward to so I choose him.

Friday arrives and I feel a small frisson of anticipation. Brad-alike and I meet up and get on sufficiently well for me to drink myself horizontal. He's quite fanciable, but the problem is he's also Jewish. Instead of wanting to rip his clothes off and ravish him, I want to take him home and make him chicken soup. Another Bloody Mary solves the problem: ravish it is.

My masculine side endorses this behaviour while my feminine side weeps and wails and rents her clothing. I go through the motions of having a great time, but it's the wrong time, the wrong place and though his face is lovely . . . well, you know the rest.

His persistent and diligent ministering to the temple of my moistness affords me little bliss. I feel detached and guilty and instead of enjoying him for what he is (a 24-year-old stud with the strongest biceps I've ever kneaded) I fantasize that it's The

Right Man making love to me. This makes me cry – tears of nostalgia, sorrow and regret – and I hastily turn my face away into the pillow. All in all, my attempt to have a zipless fuck *à la* Erica Jong fails miserably and leaves me feeling hollow and empty. Before I fall asleep I lie in bed remembering something TRM said: that he couldn't have sex without love. Although I can, and often do, it just so happens that I rather wouldn't.

The next day I meet up with Terry, my old cabinet-maker, and between us we concoct a design for a laptop case with an integrated cigar humidor. Very special, very exclusive.

Just as we're refining the details, my mobile rings and distracts me. I glance down at the screen to see who is calling – It's The Right Man! I can't believe it! I'm itching to answer the phone but somehow manage to stop myself.

'Let's make up three samples in mahogany, walnut and rosewood,' I suggest hurriedly to Terry. Whatever veneers we use, I know he'll do a fabulous job.

Then I hastily turn back to my phone to verify the missed call. It was definitely TRM. I ring him straight back but it goes to voicemail. He's obviously leaving me a message so I start doing the same to him and this goes on for the next few minutes, like some French farce restoration comedy.

He eventually comes out of the closet as I emerge from the drawing room and we crash into each other in the conservatory. He tells me that he hasn't been very well lately and apologizes profusely for not getting back to me. And then WE MAKE A DINNER DATE FOR NEXT SATURDAY!

Although I'm slightly confused by this sudden change of heart, I'm also ecstatically happy. This is it, I think to myself. I'm

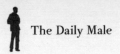 The Daily Male

definitely going to get him this time. As my heart soars like an eagle in my chest, the elation causes me to turn back to Terry and give him a great big smacker on his unexpecting cheek. He blushes crimson and looks at me in astonishment. In the thirty years I've known him, I've never kissed him once. But the fact is, at this moment, I am OVER THE MOON – so far over the moon that I'm actually sitting on God's lap, twiddling his beard and feeding him my last Rolo.

Twenty-Two

I t's Friday: the morning of the day before our next date. I make myself a healthy smoothie with all the goodies currently vegging in my fridge: ginger, blueberries, melon, carrots, orange, echinacea and goldenseal. I may have a convoluted love life but boy, am I zinging!

I spend the morning planning a research trip to Ecuador. There's an Art Biennal I want to attend showcasing up-and-coming Latin American artists. This would provide some useful material for my book and give me a chance to get away somewhere exotic under the guise of work. I won't go if things progress well with TRM, though, but maybe I need to switch my brain to another channel for a change . . .

So engrossed in my travel arrangements am I that I forget my phone is charging in the other room. When I go to find it, I notice a missed call. *Number withheld*, it says ominously. Convinced it's TRM calling to cancel, I debate whether to listen to the voicemail or chuck the phone down the loo. Some kind of crazy logic tells me that if I don't receive the message, he didn't send it.

Curiosity gets the better of me, so expecting the worst, I listen with sinking heart to his overly cheerful voice saying, 'I have a bit of a problem for tomorrow . . . '

I knew it. I bloody knew it! All hopes for the future plummet like a shot bird but he quickly explains there's someone coming to town he simply has to see, but as an alternative to tomorrow, he could make tonight or, failing that, Sunday lunch instead.

'Sunday lunch?' I shout out loud. 'Sunday bloody lunch!' A Saturday night date is very different in my world to a Sunday Bloody Sunday lunch!

I call him back and he actually answers. Though I know it sounds desperate, I tell him that tonight is fine. I was going to the dress rehearsal of a new production of *Oliver!* but bugger that. For The Right Man, it seems, *I'd Do Anything* . . .

I check my watch and realize I only have four hours to go. Four hours! I immediately put all other jobs aside and begin the gargantuan task of Getting Ready. I try on the new slinky black dress with the gold belt, without the gold belt, with the pearls, without the pearls, with the silver necklace, with the gold beads, with the chain belt, without the chain belt, with all of them together, with none of them at all, until I'm so fed up with myself I just want to put on my jimjams and go to bed.

I rummage through my overstuffed wardrobe and realize I haven't a thing to wear. I look through my summer clothes and pull out a sundress, which I try it on with a jumper underneath. Then I put on a lace vest teamed with a business suit. Then a severe skirt with a frivolous top. I'm starting to panic now. I hate everything I own. I'm going to give it all away. My room looks like an explosion in a Lost Luggage shed. I return to the new black dress with no belt and the silver necklace. It'll have to do. I arrange my hair so that it looks smart yet sexy and put on my killer heels. It's 6.30 p.m. I'm ready with half an hour to spare.

By 6.45 p.m. I'm absolutely bricking it. If I put any more make up on, I'll look like Priscilla, Queen of the Desert. I need a drink, but I don't want to smell of alcohol. I win then lose the same argument and pour myself a vodka with cranberry juice which I knock back in one gulp. I pick up the bottle then put it down again.

At 7.10 p.m. I pour myself another drink.

At 7.15 p.m. my phone rings. I grab it off the kitchen table. It's him. He can't make it. No, it's OK. He's apologizing. He sounds incredibly stressed. He's running late. He'll be another five minutes.

'No problem!' I squeak brightly and take a neat slug from the bottle.

You can be five years late, darling, as long as you turn up eventually.

I check myself one more time in the mirror. Short of stripping everything off and starting again, there's not much else I can do.

Another few minutes pass, during which I develop a tic in my right eye. I can feel it flickering uncontrollably. Now I'm slightly tipsy and my eye's all a-quiver. I begin to worry that I'm going to break both ankles tottering down the stairs. This heels-vodka combo could be a killer. Oh well, I think, at least then I could claim disability allowance and retire quietly to Eastbourne where I won't have to worry about dating The Right-or-Wrong Man any more.

Unable to contain myself any longer, I pick up my bag and keys and walk very carefully down the three flights of stairs. I wait in the hallway juddering like I've left my engine running until eventually a black cab pulls up outside. I take a deep breath, stick my chest out, pull my stomach in and step out through the door. And then I'm smiling and walking confidently towards him, almost as if a film director's just cried, 'Action – you're on!'

He's in the back of the taxi on his mobile phone. He grasps my hand as I climb in and pulls a face of apology. Lord! It's really him. He's wearing a crisp white shirt, a grey suit and no tie. He's looking very handsome! I haven't seen him since that last awful night and he actually seems to have improved. Funnily enough, the illusion I've created in my mind never focuses on his looks. It's more about his complexity and the way he makes me feel – or *made* me feel when 'love was young'.

He finishes his call and turns to me and we give each other a big hug and a kiss on each cheek. Then he looks me up and down, and smiles. I smile back demurely; I'm glad I didn't wear the tacky gold belt.

'You look absolutely gorgeous,' he says, running his eyes all over me with undisguised admiration. Then he releases my hand suddenly as if holding on to it any longer might lure him back to some dark and painful place.

'It's all new,' I reply, so glad he noticed. 'Especially for tonight.' I bestow upon him the sunshine of my warmest smile.

He apologizes again for being late then draws my attention to the fact that his shoes could have been cleaner.

'But you've been working,' I say, helping him to excuse himself. I wouldn't have cared if he'd been wearing one beaded flip-flop and a Wellington boot. In my eyes, this man can do no wrong.

'I wanted to go home and change,' he continues in a *poor-me* kind of way, 'but I ran out of time. In fact, I nearly had to cancel, but I knew that wouldn't have gone down too well!'

Too bloody right it wouldn't.

'To be honest, I've not been well again since we last met. Bad back . . . ' he whines, stretching and putting his hand on his sacrum.

183

'You look very well now,' I say affectionately. 'How do you feel?'

He doesn't reply. Instead he looks straight ahead, seemingly lost in his own thoughts. His hands are now clasped tightly in his lap. I want to take one of them in mine and lift it to my lips but I really don't dare. There seems to be a barrier between us. Suddenly my mind fills with the sexploits I described so vividly in *The Toyboy Diaries* and the adventures I've also had since he and I met. I wonder if he's read the book yet. I doubt he'd be here if he had. As the worry invades my mind, I can't think of a single thing to say to him. The unmentioned *chef d'oeuvre* hangs between us like a bad smell. Tension fills the air.

As soon as we're seated in the restaurant the atmosphere changes, however. He orders two glasses of champagne, we clink a toast and relax into conversation, just like two normal people out on a normal date. We share a bottle of wine with the meal. I know I'll have a headache in the morning but what the heck? I don't need my head for anything other than thinking about him – and that's meant *pain* for the past five weeks anyway.

During the evening, he compliments me on everything: the colour of my lipstick, my matching nail varnish, my dress, my necklace, my earrings – every detail of what I'm wearing. If I didn't know better, I'd think he was gay. I begin to regain my confidence, to recapture the feeling of security I felt when we first met.

Every now and then I refer back to our holiday, to the lovely times we shared together. 'And oh, that wonderful afternoon . . . ' I sigh.

He coughs and fiddles with his shirt. He will not meet my eye. I notice a button hanging loose from the cuff of his jacket, and another one actually missing. I point them out to him, fussing like the Jewish mother that I am.

'You need someone to look after you,' I offer devotedly. 'If you want to come home with me after, I'll sew them back on for you.'

Come here, little boy, I have a bag of sweets.

'We'll see,' he says somewhat reluctantly. 'Maybe . . . but I can't stay late.'

I experience a wave of irritation. *For God's sake!* Seducing this man is like trying to get a Mother Superior to masturbate in front of the Pope to the soundtrack of 'Hey Big Spender'.

He is pulling at his sleeve now, trying to turn it round so I won't see, and his eyes are hangdog as he looks at me. 'You'll tell all your friends I arrived late looking like a tramp,' he moans.

'Don't be silly!' I answer. 'I'll tell them that you arrived on a white charger looking tall and gorgeous and that we had a wonderful evening. That's right isn't it?' I'm sounding like Sensible now.

And once again it's me who feels insecure. I'm trying to love the pants off him and he's imploding before my eyes like a puppet whose strings have been cut. What *is* it with this man?

However, when we eventually climb into a cab and give directions to my flat, he takes my hand at last. I seize the moment of intimacy and entwine my legs through his. He looks down at my feet.

'Oh what lovely shoes!' he remarks as I snuggle up against him. He's running his hand up and down my arm now, and I feel like I'm drowning but the life raft's been left off the manifest. I sigh deeply and rest my head against his shoulder.

'There's so much I want to say to you,' I whisper. Then some hidden force gags me and I stammer to a halt. The moment passes. I've waited so long to be with him – yet now he's here, I can't express myself. The taxi pulls up outside my block, and I meet his eyes questioningly. His look tells me nothing.

'Would you like to . . . ?' I begin.

'You look after me so well,' he says, like he's leaving hospital after a long, traumatic stay.

'It's my pleasure,' I reply. 'I'd like to look after you some more . . .' and with that, I exit the cab and walk up to the front door with a confidence I don't feel. I don't dare look around but then I hear the taxi door slam shut and my pulse quickens as his footsteps follow me in.

And now I've got him, back in my flat, which is A Major Achievement. I light the candles, put on the *Gotan Project,* pour him another glass of wine and go into the kitchen to prepare some dessert.

I scoop two balls of Vanilla Toffee Crunch into my crystal bowls and top them off with Hershey's Chocolate Sauce. I sprinkle some almonds over them and take two spoons from the drawer. I get a surge of euphoria as I'm doing this: *I'm* making *him* a treat while *he* relaxes in *my* home. 'Ta dah!' I say to myself with a flourish.

When everything's ready, I return to the living room with a tray. He's lying immobile on the floor. His eyes are closed.

'I'm not dead,' he mumbles into the air as I set the tray down near him. I wonder whom he's trying to convince.

'I'm glad about that,' I answer. Then without premeditation, I stand astride him, one foot either side of his waist.

He opens his eyes and looks up at me.

'You've got me trapped,' he says, and I'm not quite sure if he's terrified or thrilled.

'Yup!' I reply.

'Look at this!' he remarks, propping himself up on an elbow and admiring the spread I've laid before him. 'You're like Mrs. Beeton in suspenders!' We both laugh and I sink down on to the floor and lay beside him.

We look into each other's eyes for a long moment and he reaches out for me and very gently, oh so gently, we begin to kiss. Oh blessed Mary Mother of God – at last! Joy and jubilation wash over me.

Suddenly he pulls away and sits up. I recoil in surprise, my stomach crashing through me like a broken lift through a burning building. He notes my hurt expression and quickly takes my hand.

'It's not that I don't want you, or that I don't fancy you,' he says. 'I think you're the sexiest woman that ever walked the earth. I have masturbated thinking about you every single day since we met. This just doesn't fit in with my life, you see . . . the way I have got used to living . . . '

For a long while, I don't trust myself to speak.

'Being alone is your comfort zone, isn't it?' I say eventually. 'I knew that all along, but I thought if maybe you'd been willing to let me in, I could have changed that . . . or changed myself, somehow. Worked something out . . . something you would have felt comfortable with . . . '

He shakes his head resignedly. 'I know myself too well.'

Despite his repeated rejection of me, I lean over and put my arms around him. He holds me close with so much tenderness that I cannot believe he doesn't want me. We begin to kiss again and his desire for me is unmistakable. I feel the force of him against my body and I know now that I've got him. At least for tonight. I stand up and reach out my hand for his and step in the direction of the bedroom. Not without difficulty, he gets up.

'I need to pee,' he says. 'But I have hydraulic problems!'

'Don't pee on my ceiling!' I warn good-humouredly and proceed down the corridor like a high-heeled Julius Caesar returning home to victory.

He comes into the bedroom carrying the tray. I'm posing in my lingerie denying the earlier words he'd said. I can't think about them now. I must cherish this moment. It may not come again. He puts the tray down on the bed and I roll onto my tummy and start spooning the mixture into my mouth. Then I turn onto my back and drizzle a large glob of ice cream and chocolate sauce into the space between my breasts. He emits a low moan then kneels down and begins to lap at it, slowly at first, then more rapaciously. He pulls his clothes off and climbs up beside me, worshipping my body like a celebrant praying at a temple he must soon destroy.

At 11.45, I usher him out of bed. He's already told me he must be home by midnight. I want him to stay with me but tonight my behaviour must be beyond reproach.

'Come on, Cinderfella,' I say, helping him to find his clothes. Then, 'When will I see you again?' spills from my mouth as he puts on his shoes and socks.

'Well,' he answers slowly, 'I'm not sure. It's my birthday soon, so . . . '

'Would you allow me the pleasure of cooking you dinner?' I croon like some faded *chanteuse* singing yet another encore.

And next time your car is dirty, I'll lick the road kill off your tyres.

'I'll call you,' is his answer, and not for the first time, I plunge into the mire of thinking: *When? When?*

As I lead him past the bookcase towards the door, I pray he doesn't glance over my shoulder to where *The Toyboy Diaries* sits face-out on the shelf.

He kisses me on the cheek, squeezes my hand, kisses me on the mouth then leaves. The bleeding heart I wear on my sleeve drips plasma all over my dressing gown.

I cling to the hope that he'll be back, and soon. No man can adore a woman's body the way he just did mine and walk away. Can they?

Before I climb back into bed, I text him: *It was lovely spending time with you. I hope we can do it again soon x*

Kill him with kindness and if that doesn't work . . . just kill him.

Twenty-Three

Ten days pass and I hear nothing from him. I imagine him holed up in some eyrie somewhere, looking out over a wild and windblown sea, tormented and alone like Lord Byron before his suicide. I quell my daily urge to call him and decide to leave him be. If he's alone, it's because he wants to be.

The day of his birthday arrives. I didn't pursue spending it together. Instead I sent him a romantic card that took me several hours to choose. At lunchtime, just as I'm making myself some cheese on toast, my mobile rings. I reach for it and say 'Hello?' without checking who it is.

'I just wanted to thank you for your birthday card,' says TRM's voice pleasantly.

'You've very welcome,' I answer intimately, trying not to do a triple somersault and land with my face on the grill. 'Did you relate to it like I did?'

This question is greeted with a crashing silence that tells me he hasn't even read the printed message, let alone my hand-written one. I search around in my mouth for something that doesn't sound like a garotted woman gargling with anti-freeze.

'So what are you doing with the rest of your special day? And evening?' I add nosily.

He tells me he's taken the afternoon off as he's got a doctor's appointment.

'This is obviously the future for me now I'm 47,' he says somberly. 'It'll be varicose veins next, then haemorrhoids, then the inevitable prostate problems. Any time off in future will be spent pounding the pavements of Harley Street.'

He delivers this in a dry tone tinged with humour, but I know there's an underlying fear behind it. Because of the way he tells it, though, I giggle girlishly at every word. Haemorrhoids and prostate are no laughing matter but coming from him? Hilarious! The fact is I'm overwhelmed to be having such a normal conversation with him.

Then he suddenly says, 'Speak soon, got to go,' and abruptly hangs up.

I stand there wondering if he really made the call or if I'd wishfully imagined the whole thing.

The weekend comes around, and a Sunday supper is arranged with the Sisterhood.

The girls are ambivalent when we meet in the evening and I bring them up to speed on the latest developments.

'Talk about messing her about!' comments Sensible to the rest of the crew. 'Why does she put up with it? She's worth more than that. Can't she see he's just using her whenever he fancies sex?'

Half Empty (no longer Full) nods in agreement.

'I hate men!' repeats Blondie. 'I'm thinking of turning lesbian or celibate. Far less complicated. What did you think of him?' she turns to Calm. 'You met the bloke, didn't you?'

Calm nods affirmatively and takes a long, slow sip on her Margarita.

'He *is* an interesting man,' she says guardedly. 'Though perhaps too complicated, even for our Wendy.'

I sit there glumly wishing they wouldn't talk about me as if I wasn't there. And for once, I'm tongue-tied. I can't defend myself and I'm unable to defend him.

'By the way,' I say suddenly, trying to divert them from my now least-favourite subject, 'I'm off to Ecuador soon. That'll make a change. I may become a conservationist in the Galápagos Islands, set up home with a thousand-year old turtle. He won't be going anywhere in a hurry, and even if he does, I should be able to catch him.'

And then, for no particular reason, I burst into tears. The girls stare at me, then at each other, and leap into action.

'Double decaf cappuccino with lots of chocolate on top, please,' calls Sensible to a passing waiter.

'She really does need to get a grip,' Half Empty mutters solemnly.

'Let her cry him out,' shushes Blondie taking my hand and stroking it, which only makes me whimper more.

Calm is supportive, as always, telling me I'm amazing, not to let him diminish me, that it was never going to work between us, that he's much too screwed-up, has too many issues and it's been way too stressful for way too long.

'But what about my happy ending?' I blub into a scrunched-up tissue. 'This is the man I've hung all my dreams upon . . .'

'Darling, I'm going to be brutal here,' Calm takes the floor and everyone listens. 'Those dreams are yours, not his. You're just projecting your needs onto him. He's not responsible for your *happy-ever-after*. Listen to the silence: *his* silence. He doesn't want you. He doesn't want anyone. He just wanted a holiday romance and that's what you both got. Cut your losses and move on. But move on in a good way. No more TRM and no more toyboys! They're not the route to happy-ever-after either!'

'TRM tricked me,' I say bitterly. 'He made me believe we could be something . . .'

'No. He did not.' Calm interrupts. 'You made yourself believe that.'

'Maybe you're not destined for love anymore,' Half Empty says. 'You've stood at the altar twice and neither time did that work out. And all those failed relationships . . . maybe you're just doomed to spend your life alone . . . like I am . . .'

I don't want to hear this. I don't want to hear any of it. I hold my palm up in the air as if to say 'enough is enough', and we go on to talk about other people's stuff.

On the way home I try to analyze exactly what is going on. The release of *The Toyboy Diaries* appears to have been one catalyst for TRM's not accepting me. But why should I be so hung up on someone who disapproves of me so much? I'm not ashamed of anything I've done. I've never hurt anyone in my pursuit of hedonism and my decision to air my stories publicly has bought me the attention that I've often craved.

And then I get angry again: I never tried to dupe TRM as he duped me, pretending to be someone I'm not, making me fall in love with him then telling me he can't cope with it. What sort of a man behaves like that? Someone so afraid of dying they've forgotten how to live? At least I'm honest and making the most of the time I have left, not shrinking away from it in case, God forbid, I might enjoy myself! And who is *he* to judge me anyway?

♀

Another week goes by. I keep myself occupied with cinema, theatre and dinner outings with male and female friends, none of which amounts to a hill of beans. When my theatre group meets up this time, I spend the evening getting to know Graymond better. He's funny and intelligent and we get on well, but I'm not really that into him. It's just a ploy to pass the time until I hear from TRM again.

On the Saturday, before leaving home for Poppy's as she's got the family coming round, I sit down at the computer to firm up my plans for Ecuador. I may as well go now. Researching hotels and flights, I decide to treat myself to a Business Class ticket but as my cursor hovers over the 'Book Now' button, I bottle out, sigh and close my laptop. I don't really want to go anywhere until I know exactly *where* I am with TRM.

Unwilling to let the gap between us widen yet again, I decide to place some bait on my feminine fishing line. If I can't reel him in with this tempting titbit, I'll simply have to try another tack.

Following a shopping spree to a certain lingerie store, the pleasure of your company is requested to a very private performance of 'Mrs Beeton and the Black Lace Basque' at your earliest convenience. RSVP ASAP. Dress: optional xxx

Not long after, my phone vibrates: *Mmm . . . very hard thinking about you. Diary is being rearranged. Free tonight? x*

OH. MY. GOD. It worked! It fucking worked! Now I'll actually have to go out and buy something. I had no intention of investing in some overpriced dental floss unless it was absolutely necessary. It's now 3 p.m. and I'm not about to cancel on my family, not even for him.

Family bonding tonight, I text back. *Could do next Tues or Thurs?*

Another half an hour passes. This guy's sense of urgency goes from 'amble' to 'full stop', but when eventually an answer comes through, it's worth waiting for.

Please can I see my beautifully basqued Mrs. Beeton on Tuesday. I will relish the thought with hardened anticipation x

Followed by:

PS: Have I told you how VERY much I want you? x

Swelled up with exaltation and feeling triumphant, I go on a texting splurge with: *I am utterly yours, my darling, for as long as – and in whichever way – you want me x*

That, of course, shuts him up. Nothing like a nice doormatty message for a man to wipe his feet all over before walking away.

On the Sunday I find myself with a clearer head and feeling stronger. I have high hopes for Tuesday, determined, yet again, to make TRM find me irresistible. Come what may, I plan to make the most of our next evening with a romantic little *diner à deux*.

I do a food shop and some yoga. Then I give my wardrobe a good clear out and make up three carrier bags for charity.

That evening, torrential rain having dissuaded me from going for a poker lesson with my old mate Roger, I come to rest on my sofa and switch the TV on to find the film *Titanic* has just started. A feeling of satisfaction surges through me and I settle down for a couple of hours of vicarious thrills at the expense of Kate and Leonardo.

Just when the film is at a crucial point, a text message comes in. The disturbance is mildly irritating, but when I see TRM's name on the screen, the corners of my mouth turn up in anticipation. An unprovoked, unsolicited, spontaneous text from the man I love! I smile excitedly but as I begin to read, my face falls. The blood drains from my head, and a silent scream escapes my throat. What am I reading? What have I done?

It seems clear you will not change your ways. I have read your book and all the press. I know more details than I care to reveal. You have lied to me. I am so angry with you. For my own sanity I must say goodbye with a very sad heart. I feel very foolish for believing you.

In the yet-to-be-written *Great Tragedies of All Time*, I know this story won't get a mention. It will not rank as globally significant or even moderately important. No one got hit by a meteor, nuked by a missile, kidnapped by aliens, washed away in a tsunami or sucked into a geological fault line. But at this moment, my rattled brain feels like it has been struck by a well-aimed baseball bat.

My mobile slips from my hand as I stare blindly into space. My eyes are drawn back to the film to see the great and hopeful ship sink below the surface. My great and hopeful ship is sinking too, and I'm about to drown in the freezing depths of my own making. With trembling hand, I dial TRM's number. I've no idea what I will say because I know I'm guilty. Guilty, yes – but of what? Leading an unconventional life? Cheating on TRM with Hot Frog before we even had a relationship? Seeking solace with Brad-a-like when TRM said he didn't want me? Being lunged at by Eurotrash and managing to fend him off? Looking for love in all the wrong places? Falling in love with all the wrong men?

The phone goes straight to voicemail. 'I just got your text,' I croak. 'I don't know what to say. Please tell me what's happened to make you feel this way? If it's something in the papers, you know they lie. Please call me. Please. Don't let it end like this . . .'

Over the next two hours, I dial his number repeatedly, leaving increasingly frantic messages. At 11.53 p.m., my mobile trills and a surge of adrenaline shoots through me. It's going to be him and it's going to be OK; he wouldn't be calling if it wasn't going to be OK.

His voice slashes my ear like a razor blade. 'What do you want?' he snaps.

'*You're* calling *me*,' I whimper.

'I'm returning your calls because you're driving me nuts.'

'Oh.'

I attempt some self-serving explanation – some fucked-up farce of fact and fiction. I know I'm losing him more with every word, though. He says it's not the book or the press but something else. Then he falls silent. I beg him to tell me what he's talking about.

'I will not reveal my source,' he says in a steely, grating voice like some faceless Gestapo interrogator.

And then he takes his turn. And he takes it like a prize fighter, bursting into the ring with both arms flailing. He slams me against the ropes with his hatred and disdain, pounding into me until I can't take any more. But I stay on the line, listening to every word.

'You're nothing but a cheap whore!' he shouts. 'How dare you even talk to me! Peddling your filth all over town! Selling the press your dirty little stories! And as for *inspiring other women*! Huh! Who in their right minds would be inspired by you? You deceived me into thinking your past was over, but you've been carrying on just like before!'

He pauses for a moment like he's reflecting if that's enough but then he begins again. I know I should hang up, but I feel too shocked to move and although his hatred is pulsating down the line, I cannot bear to break this final link. I let him go on and on relentlessly battering me with his verbal vitriol until I feel totally broken. Eventually, sounding quite exhausted, he runs out of steam.

'I don't need this any more and I certainly don't need *you*,' he says finally. 'No. Thank. You. I'm going to say goodbye now.'

I remain silent. I can't talk.

This non-relationship I've worked so hard at bending, shaping, moulding and twisting into something we could both be happy with, is disintegrating in my hand.

'Say goodbye!' he commands harshly, breaking my thought process. 'Be polite to me at least!'

'I can't,' I gasp. 'I can't say goodbye. Anyway,' I ask in the tiniest voice possible, 'what's so good about goodbye?'

I expect him to hang up but he doesn't. Instead he starts berating me again, shouting that I am a disgrace to womanhood and telling me to take A Long Hard Look at Myself.

'You know what the saddest thing is?' he says finally. 'I thought I'd found one of the most beautiful, clever, witty and sexy women in the world. And then you turn out to be like *this*.'

I'm lying in the rubble now. His words wash over me like the aftershocks of an earthquake.

For no apparent reason – maybe light-headedness because I'm not breathing properly – I suddenly begin to see the funny side. He's sounding like a cross between Cardinal Wolsey and

Miss Jean Brodie. A snigger escapes my mouth. I place the phone on the table and go to forage for my emergency fags. I light one, indifferent as to whether he hears or not. I close my Dupont with a satisfying clunk and sit back down like a convict enjoying his final smoke.

When I pick up the phone again, TRM is still ranting. I wait for a pause before I interrupt.

'I suppose Tuesday's off then?' I ask flippantly. After all, what have I got to lose?

He doesn't get the irony. 'YES! It's OFF! OF COURSE IT'S OFF!'

I get more daring then because I know there's no way back. 'You may despise me now,' I say, 'but I was good enough for you to wank over for the last few months, wasn't I?'

'I am going now,' he states grimly.

This is my last chance. I speak with great difficulty, but speak I do because suddenly, I really mean it. 'I just want to tell you how much I love you.'

The words he may have longed to hear at some point in his life, delivered now too little, too late, by the person he least wishes to hear them from, are greeted with a stony silence.

And that is it. Slowly I flip my phone shut. I sit there rigid unable to move. I light another cigarette and wonder what just happened. Then grief wraps itself around me like a rotten, putrid blanket. I feel ravaged; like a character in fast frame which has aged a hundred years. I shrink into the sofa and sob helplessly into my hands.

At some time around two in the morning, moving like a zombie, I drag myself off the sofa and get ready for bed: make-up off, face cream on, nightie. I can't bear to look at myself in the mirror lest the tears begin again. The beginnings of another migraine throb gently like a waiting taxi just above my right eye.

I don't know how many nails an average coffin needs but I'm sure there's always room for one more.

I'm about to switch my mobile off when a text bleeps in. I sit bolt upright. It could be him – The Right Man – writing to apologize. I scramble around for my phone but it's not him. I don't know who it is. When I thought my love life was sorted, I deleted the numbers of all past lovers so I don't recognize the one that comes up. I open the message. Ah. I do however recognize the tone.

Wat u up 2? Ive got the raging horn again. Shall I cum over? Hehe.

Cute Face. I never thought I'd hear from *him* again.

He's obviously pissed and seeking – as they say – *any port in a storm*. I'm fairly certain he's done the geography and my particular port is the closest to the bar he's just fallen out of, not to mention the gutter he's about to fall into. It's 2 a.m. I've had the shittiest evening ever, and the last thing I fancy is being used as a doughnut for some young buck's pleasure.

He texts me again: *You there babe?*

I don't even need to think about this one. *NO*, I text firmly. *You want a fuck? You can fuck off!* The next minute he's on the line, trying to convince me. He is very drunk and when I refuse once again he becomes abusive.

'Come on,' he says meanly, 'at your age you should be grateful.'

Grateful? Who does the little thug think he is?

'How dare you!' I say. 'Go and find someone else to be rude to.'

'Maybe I will,' he sneers. 'Someone who doesn't lie about their age. You told me you were 51 but you're not. You're fucking 61, which makes you a bloody liar!'

I'm 62 actually, I want to say, but I kill the call mid-stream and switch my phone off. His invective doesn't bother me as such, but on top of everything else, it doesn't contain the feel-good factor either. I decide in future to always tell the truth about my age. If anyone doesn't like it, they know what they can do. Wound up now by two personal attacks from two men in one night, I switch my mobile back on and text him.

Life lesson for you: calling late and drunk for a fuck then making insulting remarks is decidedly unappealing. You'll never impress a real woman like that. A little charm goes a long way. A hard cock is not enough – plenty of those on offer with nicer men attached.

Cute Face throws all his toys out the pram and huffs back: *Plenty of younger women around who don't try to take the moral high ground after they've lied about their age.*

My age didn't seem to matter, I text back, *when your head was between my legs and you still wanted to come over tonight, didn't you?*

That shuts him up.

Looking at it from his point of view, I can see where he's coming from. He's 27; I suspect that his granny may not be a million years older than me. And while a 50-year-old might be good for his street cred, a woman in her sixties tips the balance towards ladies in lavender. Nevertheless, he still phoned me up for a shag tonight knowing my real age, so go figure. When the blood has risen, any orifice will do.

♀

The rest of the night I thrash about, staring into the dark and wishing I'd never met The Right Man. Will anyone ever be right for me again? My future stretches before me in shades of monochrome. And yet, as the night turns into a chill and gloomy dawn, all the strengths of my life press themselves into being, and I salute the strong women from whom I am descended – women who walked barefoot across Russia in the ice and the snow to seek salvation in a foreign land. My crisis is nothing compared to theirs. But if they survived that, I can survive this.

As daybreak chases away the darkest of the night's demons, I agree TRM had a certain point. But he will not reduce me. I've made my bed and I'm going to lie in it with whichever lovers I choose. If he opts not be one of them then that's his loss. His inability to accept me for who I am says more about him than it does about me. And what's a man of 47 doing with no relationship history anyway?

I'll get over him, I think as I get up in the morning and paint on my public face. I've got over men before. And if anyone asks me why I live like this, my answer is: Because I Can. Who Dares Wins – not always – but at least one has to try.

Twenty-Four

How is it possible to have breakfast in England and dinner in Ecuador? Yes, I know the logistics, but I still find it amazing: 17 hours after leaving home, I'm in a completely different world.

The few days before departure were unutterably grim. I got through them with my brain on automatic but the night before the flight, as I started to pack, I went into total meltdown. My social failures marched across my mind like Mickey Mouse's broomsticks in *The Sorcerer's Apprentice*. An emergency call brought Blondie over on the run. She sat in my kitchen listening to my ranting while I scorched my way through the ironing. By the time she left, I felt a little better. And the ironing was done.

I awake on my first morning in Quito, the capital of Ecuador, not quite sure if it's half-past June or the following Tuesday. I get dressed in a bit of a daze and go down to the dining room for breakfast. The sumptuous buffet is laid out in a similar style to the one at *Club Merde*, and I get a little pang of nostalgia as I remember making eyes at The Right Man while Hot Frog prowled the perimeter. I swat these thoughts away and tell myself with steely determination that from now on I will live IN THE MOMENT.

As my stomach can't work out the time difference, I eat breakfast, lunch, tea and dinner then set off to visit the old town. A cab drops me in the main square where I soak up the *ambiente*. Then I make my way to an art exhibition being held in the Town Hall. There are hordes of local school children milling about the vast rooms, their ancestry etched in their little faces: Inca, Aztec and Indian. I feel pale and conspicuous amongst these exotic natives.

I walk through one gallery then into another until I reach a grand salon, empty save for a tall, fair-haired man standing with his back to me in the far corner. I work my way through the exhibits towards him and, as he turns, I catch my breath. He is very young, very tall, deeply tanned and totally gorgeous.

My veil of jet lag, disorientation and heartbroken misery is momentarily lifted as my inherent Wendiness kicks in. I flicker a smile at him, which he immediately returns. The words *learn, will, you* and *never* barely cross my mind.

'What is this made of?' I ask, peering curiously at a huge sheet of something knobbly suspended on the wall.

'Could be egg cartons?' he suggests in a sing-song Scandinavian accent. He looks straight at me and I all but drool into his limpid blue eyes. The rest of his face is equally good to look at: unblemished skin, a slightly turned-up nose and a full, sensuous mouth, lips parted to reveal a set of even white teeth. With his sun-streaked mane of flowing hair he looks like a handsome young lion, or a cross between David Hasselhof and George Michael in his *Wham* days.

'*Thank you God*,' I say silently, '*but wouldn't it be more constructive if you helped me not to do this any more?*'

The Beautiful Boy and I wander round the gallery together, passing comments on some of the quirkier stuff. I know I can't attach myself to him indefinitely so when we reach the final exhibits, I smile like a grown-up, say, 'Enjoy the rest of your stay,' and head for the exit.

I immediately regret having left him. My onward flight isn't until tomorrow and I've got the rest of the day and the whole of the night to kill. I wander aimlessly out into the square and sit down on a bench to study the map and ponder my next move. A minute later the Beautiful Boy materializes in the Town Hall's doorway. He pauses on the pavement looking this way and that. I stand up and take a few hesitant steps in his direction. He notices me and waves and we walk towards each other.

'I'm not sure where to go now,' I say, and my query is genuine. 'I only got here last night. I haven't even got a guide book. Any ideas? You've probably explored a bit more than I have.'

'I'm going up to the Basilica,' he answers. 'You should see it. It's the highest point in the city.'

'Mind if I walk with you?' I ask, *carpe*-ing the *diem*, and we set off together, side by side.

BB is Swedish, on the final leg of a world tour. He's off home tomorrow, back to his family in Stockholm.

We navigate the narrow, hilly, cobbled streets of the old town, until we come across a market where we buy colourful alpaca scarves and wooden whistles carved like cockatoos. At one point, I step out into the road without looking just as a rickety old bus comes hurtling round the corner towards me. He grabs my hand and pulls me back, then puts his arm protectively around my shoulder. I lean against him gasping, not because my knees have gone weak with lust, but because Quito is one of the highest cities in the world and the air is so thin it's hard to breathe. I battle on regardless, not wishing to appear old or unfit and am relieved when we stop for lunch in another pretty square. He tells me some of his traveller's tales then we talk about life and love, my past and his future. I ask him what plans he has for his last evening and to my delight, he suggests spending it with me.

As he's staying in some $5-a-night flea pit and I'm in an all-expenses-paid, five-star hotel, I propose, with a hint of humour, that he pick up his rucksack, check out of the hostel and swing over to the swanky Sheraton. I have *two* double beds and a marble bathroom full of fluffy white towels and luxury products, I tell him. That way he can have a nice hot bath and a clean, white bed before he sets off on his journey home. My *coup de grâce* is the additional inducement of a well-stocked mini bar.

'Sounds tempting!' he laughs and clicks his back teeth. This obviously means something in Swedish – probably 'Forget it, grandma!' – and he doesn't take the bait so I don't insist.

We arrange to meet at 8.30 p.m. at the Whisky Store and I jump into a cab and head back to the hotel. I am absolutely reeling with excitement. I've only been away 24 hours and I have a date tonight with a stunningly handsome 21-year-old! I couldn't have planned it better if I'd tried. It's *Quito* Amazing.

Before leaving the hotel to meet him again, I have a flash of inspiration. I tell the Receptionist that my nephew may be in town tonight, and if I manage to find him, he'll be staying over in my room. She must think I think she's stupid! She's hotel staff, for Crissakes! Nevertheless, she smiles accommodatingly and says that'll be fine, as long as he checks in. The stage is set.

I cab it back to the centre and wait for BB at the appointed place. He arrives ten minutes late, during which time I have visions of myself propping up the bar all night, getting drunker and drunker, because the innocent young backpacker the old broad picked up in the museum failed to show and she had no alternative but to drown her sorrows in rotgut hooch. Then I see myself sliding off the bar stool onto the sawdust floor and being carted off to jail because I can't remember who I am and the local villains stole my handbag.

BB *does* turn up though, freshly laundered and even more gorgeous than before which can't have been easy. He's been on the road for the past nine months staying in crummy hostels with dubious hot water and cockroaches for company.

We sit out on a roof terrace above the bustling street and we talk and talk. He tells me how he lost his virginity age 14 to a 21-year-old with whom he had a short affair. Younger men love relating their Benjamin stories to Mrs. Robinson, and tonight, I am she.

He also talks about his girlfriend and how much he misses her. He's been faithful throughout this trip despite many opportunities and temptations, and I respect him for that. Tonight it could go either way, but far be it for me to come between a man and his fidelity! The more I look at him though, the luckier I think she is.

As he downs his fourth beer on top of two bourbon cocktails, he gets quite touchy feely and I remind him to behave and think about his Anneka, waiting patiently back in 'Shweeden'. The altitude has definitely got to me, rewiring my morals and fiddling with the switches on my sex drive.

When the night turns chilly we go inside. There's a Subbuteo table in the upstairs bar and we have an energetic game in which I acquit myself fairly well for a beginner. We also have a game of darts – another first for me – and I manage to beat him, but then I *am* a lot more sober.

The street is teaming when we spill out at 1 a.m. and we hang around on the corner wondering what to do next. I know exactly what I'd like to do but I decide not to push it. I've had a fantastic day and evening and I shall send him on his way with fond memories of me. As we're about to say goodbye, he suddenly asks how old I am.

'Guess!' I say laughing.

'48?' he asks. 'Maybe 50?'

I tell him my truth and he nods admiringly.

'Cool,' he says. 'I'll tell my mum I had a date with a woman who's older than she is!'

'But you won't tell your girlfriend, will you?' I tease and he shakes his head, hugs me tightly and kisses me goodbye.

I give him my email address, which he's bound to forget, and he puts me into a taxi. We wave until we're out of sight. Then I gaze up at the starry sky, thank the Latin-American moon for having smiled on me and heave a contented sigh. I'm glad to have met him and glad we behaved. I go to bed happy wondering what tomorrow will bring.

ICARO is not, perhaps, the best moniker for a company which boasts reliability in the skies. What were those boardroom boys thinking? No matter – the flight from Quito to Cuenca was smooth, if somewhat chaotic. The locals on their way home from the capital called animatedly across the aisles to each other, sang raucous songs, shouted into their mobile phones throughout the flight and leapt out of their seats to open the overhead lockers the second the plane touched down, despite the fact that it was still hurtling along the runway at 500 miles an hour.

I arrive in the small but perfectly formed city of Cuenca late in the evening. The staff at *Mansion Alcazar* welcomes me warmly with a glass of local brew and a hot, mint-infused towel. The place is dimly lit and somewhat gloomy, and I wonder how I will survive five nights here *toute seule* after the excitement of Quito and the company of my Beautiful Boy.

I unpack my belongings and set off to explore the colonial-style hacienda. Heavy antique furniture squats menacingly in every corner; vast oil paintings of aristocratic ancestors glare critically down at me from on high. An ornately tiled fountain decorated with bowers of flowers tinkles in the centre of the large indoor patio. It's right outside my ground-floor window. I hope they turn that off at bedtime, I think to myself, or I'm going to want to pee all night. (Mercifully, they did, so I didn't.)

There's a small library upstairs adjoining what must once have been the formal dining room. Sitting quietly on one of the settees is a grey-haired *gringo* leafing through a volume of wildlife photos. I nod politely at him and to my surprise he answers with a 'How do?' He's a doctor from Yorkshire travelling with his son en route to Galápagos! Although I love to mingle with the locals, I'm also pleased to have British company. We agree to dine together the following night.

The next morning dawns bright and clear and I set off to explore the city. As I walk the cobbled streets, admiration for this little jewel of a place fills my heart. Who would have thought that in the southernmost part of what is essentially a Third World country on the west coast of Latin America, one would find a town of such charm and beauty? No wonder UNESCO declared it a World Cultural Heritage site – they ought to wrap it in cotton wool and preserve it forever.

The low-built houses are reminiscent of Havana but better maintained. Ornamental wrought-iron balconies grace the shuttered windows, which are framed with elaborate plaster mouldings; paintwork is ochre, pistachio or pale blue, and the solid wooden doors are studded with iron or brass. Yellow taxis, cars and buses toot loudly as they approach each intersection and the whole vibe is a busy buzz.

The local women show off their plumage like parrots in a clash of colourful costumes: full skirts in hues of fuchsia, electric blue, emerald green, turquoise and acid yellow are hand-embroidered and worn with beaded blouses, knitted cardigans and shawls crossed over like slings. Sleeping babies nestle contently against their mother's backs as the women go about their daily chores.

The weathered faces of the local people peek out from beneath narrow-brimmed trilby hats. These are the original panamas, so-called because the workmen who built the Panama Canal wore them to protect their heads from the sun. This is traditional craft from Ecuador, made right here in Cuenca.

I find my way to the Museum of Modern Art, a low-built, white-painted edifice which takes up one side of a beautifully landscaped square. I'm here to view and write about the ninth Biennal d'Arte. This showcases up-and-coming Latin American artists from 26 different countries. I study the eclectic mix of styles, some of which I do not understand. When it comes to art, I know what I like and I like what I know.

I make some notes then walk on through the lively town. I turn a corner and *whooooah*! There before me stands a Truly Magnificent Cathedral – a massive structure built in stone, with three tall cupolas tiled in azure blue. There's a little flower market

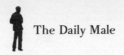

on the pavement outside: an exquisite visual palette perfumed with heady aromas. It's picture-perfect.

I buy a candle from a street vendor and enter through a portal in the enormous studded door. What greets me inside can only be described as jaw dropping. Towering arches house alcoves crammed with statues of all the saints. Stained-glass windows in every shade tell the tales of Testaments Old and New. Glimmering brass gates as high as heaven, polished marble columns, a gleaming gold altar . . . Add to this the ethereal chanting of the choir, the ponderous pounding of the organ and the salvation-seeking solemnity of the congregation and I'm rooted to the spot. Two lone words escape my mouth. Appropriately these are 'Jesus' and 'Christ'.

It's cool and quiet and I tiptoe over to a pew and sit down. I drop my shoulders and feel myself relax. A peaceful calm envelops me. Inevitably, The Right Man returns to my thoughts and I steel myself to replay and accept his devastating last words. Later, I light the candle and I say prayers for the health and happiness of all my loved ones. I focus on the little flame flickering bravely in the vast and hallowed space and I feel a stillness surround my soul. My anger and depression slowly evaporate. I acknowledge that TRM is probably a lot less happy than I am. My disappointment and sorrow turn to pity, and I say a prayer for him too. I hope he'll find the peace he craves. See how generous I've become? One small change of continent and the voodoo doll has been discarded.

Although I rarely pray in synagogue, I am captivated by the serenity of this place and I vow to return every day of my stay. You see, I've visited Notre Dame, the Sacré Coeur, St. Paul's and St. Peter's but I can't help being more impressed by this treasured La Immaculada, tucked away as she is in a tiny town in the foothills of the Andes.

♀

The next day I awake, refreshed. I stretch out in my four-poster bed listening to the fountain tinkle delicately outside my window. It's 8 a.m. Early morning noises drift across the patio as the house wakes up, preparing for another day. The heavenly strains of the Hallelujah Chorus soar through the strategically positioned speakers. I feel more at peace in this remote town than I have been in a long, long time. All the stresses and strains of London life have drifted away, and I'm enjoying the tranquillity and solitude more than I ever thought possible.

I spend the next few days researching and exploring, writing notes for the book and dining with the good doctor and his son. Morning and evening, I go to the cathedral. I light candles, give thanks for my blessed friends and family and say special prayers for The Right Man and his future happiness.

Back at the Mansion, I'm delighted to receive an email from my gorgeous backpacker, home in Stockholm now. I'm glad I didn't make a move on him. It's good to feel self-righteous for a change. I send him a chatty reply, telling him how my trip is going and mentioning that if ever he – and his girlfriend! – need a place to stay in London, my spare room is available.

Over dinner on their last night, the doctor and his son tell me about their visit to a Shaman in the hills. They highly recommend this trip – 'to exorcise your demons and realign your chakras' – and I decide to go. It will be another step in the journey towards a better, calmer me. They leave at dawn the next morning. I hope to get chatting to someone else before long. I don't mind the days by myself – in fact I love them – but I don't relish the thought of dining on my own.

That evening I arrive back at the hotel, write up my notes, shower, change and enter the dining room alone. A smartly dressed woman is sitting with a little girl, and a middle-aged couple and three lone men are all placed at separate tables. I am shown to a table for four, from which the waiter removes the other three place settings. I study the menu and order my meal, happy to note that I am feeling quite contained and, dare I say it, quietly complete.

The middle-aged couple are English and sounding quite jolly, on their second bottle of wine. When they get up to leave, they smile and nod as they pass my table. I smile back and they stop by to chat. I invite them to sit down and they immediately order another bottle of wine. We spend the rest of the evening together. They're a charming couple from Oxford; very posh, very pissed. We arrange to dine together the following night.

I turn in early and forget to switch my mobile off. It rings at 4 a.m. and I leap out of bed to kill the call. It says 'unknown' and I don't care who it is. I've been six days without texting or calling anyone, apart from the essential *arrived safely* messages to the children. Tomorrow I'll email my friends to tell them of my whereabouts.

Or maybe I won't.

On my last day I hire a guide and head out of Cuenca towards the Pan-American Highway. We pass through a couple of villages, their colourful markets bursting the seams of the central square. We stop by a farm where a woman makes shawls and watch her weaving the dyed wools into traditional Aztec designs. I buy a beautiful black and white one I know I'll keep forever. She also breeds guinea pigs in a ramshackle outhouse. Guinea pigs are not pets in Ecuador, but a delicacy to be sold to the finest restaurants.

They come in different shades of white, cream, brown, grey and black, and some are piebald. They climb all over each other when she opens the cages and mate indiscriminately and incestuously, judging by their numbers. They're quite cute but I'm not sure I could eat a single one, never mind a whole family.

At the tiny town of Chordoleg, we stop near the market square where the healers' tents have been set up. This is our final destination: the place the *curanderas* come to cure their clients of their ills and woes.

As I walk towards the tents, a tiny woman, no taller than a child, beckons me over. I couldn't begin to guess her age: she could be 35, she could be 70. I sit down on a low stool and she tips some oily liquid into the palm of her hand and starts to smear it all over my face.

'*Cuidado con mi maquillaje, por favor!*' I cry with an apologetic smile. This make-up took me a while . . . please be careful not to smudge it!

She mutters something I don't understand – probably 'you vain cow, this'll never work' – then picks up a bundle of herbs and grasses and sets about beating me over the head with them. She mumbles and spits as she whacks me everywhere – not an inch of my body escapes the wrath of her herbal flagellation.

I close my eyes and try to get into it, but the guide is busy taking photos, which I find rather distracting. I'm also trying not to laugh – the whole process is so bizarre, it's making me nervous. The *curandera* then discards the spent grasses and rubs me all over with a hen's egg, muttering all the while. She breaks the egg into a clear plastic cup and shows me the cloudy swirls in the glutinous white. It's the evil she's drawn out of me, apparently: all the negativity of which I had *bastante* – enough.

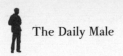

I look into the cup and nod sagely but I can't help thinking, 'Doesn't an egg white always look like that?'

The placebo effect seems to work though as I do feel rather heady as I pay my dollar and thank her respectfully. Then, oven-ready as I am, brushed with oil and dusted with herbs, I return to Cuenca, finish my souvenir shopping, visit the Cathedral one last time and then head, somewhat sadly, back to the hotel.

As I pass through the indoor patio, clutching my purchases and swathed against the chill night air in my lovely Aztec shawl, I bump into the English couple. It's 4.30 p.m. so we sit down for tea. We're still talking at 10 p.m., telling each other our life stories, during which time they've consumed two cocktails apiece, three bottles of wine and are now on the champagne. (Oh! The Brits abroad . . .) I've had two Bloody Marys, which is pretty much my limit. After some soup and a salad for dinner, we exchange email addresses and kiss goodbye. They too leave early in the morning.

It's a marathon 18-hour journey home. As I sit in the airplane and think about my trip, I feel buoyed up somehow. The people I've met, the places I've been, the adventures I've had, have all filled me with a renewed sense of hope and self-confidence. So, too, has the time I've spent alone – that has been especially rewarding. I've expunged those wretched men from my thoughts and I feel so much better for it. I eject the remaining few out over the Atlantic and vow that I'll be a more composed person in the future.

Twenty-Five

The day after returning home, with a ton of work to catch up on, I awake to find my internet is down. This is mildly inconvenient – LIKE HAVING BOTH ARMS CUT OFF AT THE ELBOW AND BOTH LEGS AT THE KNEE! I try not to panic as I struggle with strangers in Bangalore who talk to me in tongues using words like 'protocol', 'logfile' and 'encryption'. A migraine circles my head like a hungry scavenger then dive bombs into the side of my skull causing my own hard drive to crash. Every time I move my head I see the full Aurora Borealis accompanied by The Royal Philharmonic Orchestra playing Stravinsky at full blast. I have no alternative but to take some head drugs and go to bed.

With the curtains closed, tucked beneath the duvet, my mind roams aimlessly through the labyrinth of my life. I encounter The Right Man tap-dancing his way through my frontal lobe. My Little Ponytail lounges on my cerebral cortex, and there's Cute Face, stamping his feet in the part of my brain not being bombarded by the Red Army Ensemble. So much for having chucked them all out over the Atlantic! A new woman has returned from Ecuador, but she finds she still has the old woman's problems.

The next day, still feeling fragile, I get a call from Boozy Suzy from the theatre group, her voice upbeat and expectant.

'I've got something to tell you . . . ' she enthuses and I feel her excitement coming down the wire.

'Go on,' I encourage.

'Jeremy's asked me to marry him and I've accepted!'

I pull my elation out of a very black hat. 'How wonderful . . . ' I croak. I grope for something else that's positive to say but at that moment, mercifully, her mobile rings.

'That's my *fee-on-say* now! Gotta go-ho!' she trills and I unclamp my jaw before I grind my teeth away.

Now don't get me wrong. I am genuinely delighted for her but I wouldn't want Jeremy for a pension. Despite this, a wave of envy courses through me, turning my very hair green. I quash these evil thoughts as best I can and send her a text of congratulation. I then shamble through the rest of the day, groaning and bumping into things, my bio-rhythms totally shot to hell.

Later that night, and by way of explanation, the fullest moon looms out from behind a tree. Now I know why I've been feeling so crazy! I acknowledge the moon's awesome beauty and determine to feel better tomorrow.

I spend the next day trying to clear my desk and my head. I do some yoga, make chicken soup and listen to classical music.

To my surprise, Lily pops up unexpectedly in the middle of a working day. She's just been to the doctor's, she tells me ominously. She's looking tired and pale. I give her a big hug and usher into the kitchen.

'Would you like some soup, darling?' I ask. 'You look a bit washed out. Have you been eating properly?'

'Not really . . . ' she answers, studying the coal in the fireplace hungrily as if it's a rare delicacy.

'Mum . . . ' she begins hesitantly then looks at her watch. The doorbell rings at that moment and she bounds up to answer it.

'What's going on?' I query anxiously. 'Is everything alright? Who's at the door?'

My son-in-law walks in and they stand together in the hall beaming at me. The penny still doesn't drop.

'Mum!' she says again, more positively this time. 'We've got something to tell you!'

My eyebrows rise and my mouth falls open in happy surprise.

'YES!' Lily shrieks. 'We're PREGNANT! We're going to have a baby!'

I scream with joy and rush over to hug them both. My third grandchild! I'm absolutely thrilled! We baby talk away the next hour then James helps her down the stairs like she's due at any moment. I'm bursting to tell everyone but am sworn to secrecy until after her first scan.

I spend the next few weeks feverishly typing up my notes from the Ecuador trip. It changed the way I look at art and taught me not to dismiss what I don't understand. The book on future collectibles is taking shape now but my social life is on hold as I'm fired up by work. I keep in touch with friends by phone and agree to join the guys from the theatre group on the forthcoming Bank Holiday.

Early on the Sunday morning, my pals and I drive out of London heading for the Chilterns. I do enjoy the sensory pleasures of the country. It's a beautiful day as we set off on an 8-mile walking trip, to be broken half way by lunch at the

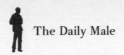

Black Boys Inn at Hurley. Graymond strides alongside me talking too loudly. His voice startles the wildlife and booms the birds off the trees.

Just as he's starting to annoy me, someone else tells him to tone it down as he's disturbing our bucolic ramble. He goes quiet and clumps along rather dejectedly. I actually feel quite sorry for him, and for once I make a real effort to talk to him.

I find a rather insecure though thoroughly kind-hearted man behind the loud façade. He tells me about his acrimonious divorce a few years ago, and his 12-year-old son who now lives in Canada. They visit each other as often as they can but the situation clearly upsets him. I realize that he craves attention to fill the gaps in his personal life. I can relate to that.

Towards the end of the afternoon, he asks me if I'd like to come over to his home one evening and he'll cook me dinner. Now that I'm seriously on the wagon – no men, not since TRM – I too have gaps in my personal life that need filling. I'm not sure I want to fill them with Graymond though, so I thank him kindly and say *maybe, soon*.

In fact, I find myself busier than expected over the next few months. Lily's ongoing pregnancy means I spend a lot of time with her, poring over baby manuals, discussing the birth plan and helping her decorate the nursery. I enjoy this Super Mum mode, cooking and organizing and trying to make Lily's transition from new wife to new mother as easy as possible. My elder daughter Poppy helps out with advice – with two births under her belt, she knows all there is to know.

The Sisterhood is not used to Celibate Wendy. They watch from the sidelines as month follows month and I remain abstinent. I don't tell them that, late at night, I dip into toyboy-warehouse.com now and then. It doesn't amount to much but messaging a bloke or two lets me know I'm still alive. I have two guys named Dan vying for my affections. I can't decide between them; either way, I'll be Dan-ned if I do and Dan-ned if I don't.

Eventually the girls organize a get-together. We haven't got together for way too long.

We meet at Sofra in St. John's Wood and we each take our turn to bring the others up to speed. I field questions about myself because, frankly, apart from work and family, there's not a lot to tell.

'It's going to close up if you're not careful,' Blondie warns.

'I used to get my booty-call bloke over when I felt that happening!' laughs Newly Single. She's the happiest of us all. She recently re-met a man she knew when she was 18 and it's all going rather well.

'Bloody men. I hate 'em but they're useful for some things,' Blondie says in her amusing, downbeat fashion.

'What about Graymond?' Sensible asks. 'You seemed to get on well together last time you met.'

'Oooh, Graymond!' coo the girls. 'The answer to a maiden's prayer – as long as you wear earplugs.'

'He's not *that* bad!' I suddenly say, jumping to his defense. 'In actual fact, I quite like him and he is, potentially, the Quintessential Older Man you would all like for me.'

Silence descends across the table. They're all smiling and nodding and for once, I smile and nod too.

♀

Graymond stays on the back burner however because one evening, I get an interesting hit on Times Encounters. In order to view his photo, I have to renew my subscription. It costs a whopping £19.99. He'd better be worth it!

My interest is piqued when I read his profile. It reminds me that I haven't been woo-ed for way too long, especially not by a 49-year-old media executive with a smart line in chat and a sexy smile. After a brief email discourse, Media Exec and I make a date for Saturday. He invites me out for dinner and then to a party afterwards. I allow myself to get a little bit excited.

When Saturday comes around though I wish I wasn't going out after all. After my Ecuadorian epiphany, I now feel capable of staying home alone without topping myself. Besides, I've got work to do preparing a brochure on the cigar humidor-come-laptop case. I want to market this worldwide as I feel it has great potential but I remind myself that it is the weekend and a girl deserves a bit of fun.

As I'm dithering over what to wear, Media Exec texts to say that the party he's taking me to has a Hawaii Five-O theme. Oh Jesus Mary and Joseph! I think I *am* going to top myself. Not only am I meeting an (older) stranger off the internet, but I now have to dress up in some horrible 1970s outfit to boot.

Before I have the chance to text him back with excuses, he informs me, *Not to worry! I've bought you some vintage stuff in Camden Market.*

Now I'm even more disgruntled. Media Exec can fuck right off. No way am I going to a party dressed in some second-hand shit that probably hasn't been washed for 30 years. In an act of thematic and social rebellion, I put on jeans and a t-shirt and wait for the bell to ring.

He arrives dead on time. The minute I set eyes on him, I know the suicide option should have been executed earlier. Despite having seen a professional photograph, the humanoid standing on my doorstep bears no resemblance whatsoever to the person on the website.

This man looks like a long-distance lorry driver: short, fat and bald with tattoos on both forearms, dressed in check slacks and a Hawaiian shirt. On his feet he wears a pair of ridiculously high yet very small-sized cowboy boots. His thighs are so heavy he has to walk with his legs apart. He looks like John Wayne, only in a fairground mirror when he's just shat himself. He may be 49, but if he's a media executive, then I'm a novice nun at the Holy Convent of the Sisters of Everlasting Chastity.

'Wendy Strawberry – 'ere's Arvey!' he cries, opening his arms wide enough for me to spot the sweat stains under each armpit. He attempts to kiss me but I flinch away. Undeterred, he marches straight into my living room, which he eyeballs approvingly, then proudly unveils a pair of cheap flowery bell bottoms and a psychedelic top, neither of which I'd wear for a bet. He's got a liberty leaving home without a license, never mind turning up at my place brandishing such items.

Tight-lipped, I refuse his repeated demands that I try them on and we go out to dinner at an Italian restaurant in Kensal Rise. The party doesn't start until 10 p.m. so we have two hours in which to get to know each other. I already know I don't want to know any more that I already know.

By the time I'm halfway through my first drink, I also know this evening is going no further than the *Veal Milanese*. His conversation is inarticulate, boring and banal and I want the evening over *now*. I pray for Lily's waters to break to save me from this torment but since she's only eight months gone, that would be another worry. I curse myself for dabbling on the internet and rack my brains to make up an excuse. As if on cue, my temple begins to throb. I give it a grateful rub.

Orrible Arvey manages to drag his attention away from his food long enough to notice my discomfort.

'What's up, love?' he bellows. 'You OK? Looking forward to the *parteeee*? We're gonna have a blast!'

'I think I've got a migraine coming on,' I whimper, my lip quivering with relief.

'Come on babe, a dance will do you good!'

'Unngh . . . ' I manage, overwhelmed with horror at the thought of being held in his sweaty embrace.

'What you sayin'?' Orrible Arvey goes on, slurping up his pasta. 'Don't tell me you don't wanna come? After all the trouble I've gone to?'

Got it in one, you ugly bugger.

'Mmmm . . . ' I mumble, eyes to the floor.

'Aw, doll. Maybe we should do this some other time?' he says gallantly, then ruins the effect by leering at my chest.

Relief surges through me like a shot of adrenaline. I apologize profusely, throw some money on the table so as not to be beholden, say goodbye and leap into a cab.

I call Blondie en route to see if she's in, pick up my car at home and shoot over to hers. At least the evening isn't totally wasted. We catch up on the news whilst bemoaning the fact of men in

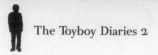

general and blind dates in particular. The threatened migraine disappears so we dispatch some vodka tonics, munch our way through a large bar of Green & Black's Butterscotch chocolate and play a couple of games of Scrabble.

Quality time is always better spent in the company of the Sisterhood.

Or alone.

Twenty-Six

After the horrendous date with Orrible Arvey, I am on yet another break from men. This doesn't bother me as such – I know I can pick the rotten darlings up any time I have a mind to. For now I have my family, my work and Lily's pregnancy to occupy me – not to mention the highs and lows of the Sisterhood which are, as ever, mixed and varied.

Newly Single is about to be Newly Wed! She and her childhood sweetheart have decided to tie the knot! Half Empty has met another future 'possible' though something tells me he'll be 'impossible' before too long. Blondie is drowning in a sea of Polish builders as she converts an investment flat. Calm is now in a relationship with the man from the brainstorming session and Sensible is sensible in every sense of the word.

Graymond keeps in touch on a regular basis and our friendship rolls along like a polished bowl on a freshly mown bowling green.

Unnoticed by me – though not by my friends – we begin to spend more time together. I invite him to a private view at Sotheby's. We amble through the auction room gawping at priceless Impressionist art. Some of the other guests are worth a look too: the cream of the international art world, plus a smattering of double-D-list titerati.

One evening, we go out to the cinema. As we're sitting in companionable silence, munching Maltesers and occasionally sniffling at the sad bits, I find myself, for some inexplicable reason, wanting to hold his hand. We're very comfortable in each other's company and despite my embargo on older men, some green shoot seems to have taken root. I'm surprised at this and spend the rest of the evening lost in thought.

As usual Gray sees me home, kisses me affectionately on both cheeks then drives away. I climb my stairs pensively wondering whether maybe one day he'll climb them with me.

Not long after, I belatedly accept his offer to cook me dinner at his home. I offer to bring a starter or a pud, but he declines.

'Graymond's cooking me dinner tomorrow night,' I tell Calm over the phone.

'Oooooh!' she answers. 'Can I hear the splatter of tiny feet?'

'Not unless he's got rats,' I reply briskly.

'Well, keep your options open,' she advises. 'One thing he won't do is mess with your head.'

'I know.' I answer. 'He's a good soul but he's just a friend, OK?' But as I hang up, I wonder if this is really, truly, still the case.

I arrive at Graymond's London residence with a bottle of Merlot and a box of Bendicks Bittermints. He welcomes me in wearing a tall chef's hat and an apron. I do a double take and peer more closely at the logo on his pinny: *Kiss the Cock?!*

I take a step backwards and read it again. Ah, it's *Kiss the Cook*, but with a smudge of something across the 'O'.

Note to self: stop being so vain and wear your glasses or you could get into serious trouble.

Although the house is lovely it needs a total revamp, preferably by someone with taste. Men who remain in the marital home after the bird has flown rarely see what they're living with. Frills and furbelows are so *passé* and my fingers itch to rip the place apart.

As my eyes scan the rooms, I mentally refurnish and redecorate. Then I follow my nose towards the enticing aromas emanating from the kitchen. I wander in and put my offerings down on the old pine table.

The room looks like a scud's hit it. Every pot, pan, dish and utensil has been brought into play and they're lying in various stages of stickiness across the formica work tops. Graymond is busy at the stove, stirring and adjusting the seasoning. I instinctively roll up my sleeves and start to tidy up. He turns to look at me and waves his wooden spoon in my direction. A glob of something gloopy flicks me in the eye.

'Ah,' he booms, 'a woman's touch! It's been a while since I've had one of those!'

I recoil slightly, hoping he's not going to jump on me, and wipe the sauce away with a piece of kitchen paper. He goes to the fridge and removes a jug of pink liquid adorned with celery sticks, which he pours into two iced glasses. The cocktail is delicious, as are the olives stuffed with anchovies and the honey-roasted cashew nuts he's laid out. Things are looking tastier and tastier. Maybe Graymond's not so Gray after all?

The evening is agreeable, even better than I expected. We talk about his work as an architect and he takes me into his office to show me a back catalogue of drawings. He's retired now but still dabbles in property. He also likes to go on self-development courses, hence the newfound cookery skills.

The cuisine, though not historic, is pretty good. He serves me a tricolore salad with fresh basil leaves, a prawn and scallop risotto flavoured with saffron and simmered in Pinot Grigio, and fresh fruit for dessert: a platter of chunked-up pieces of pineapple, mango and strawberries covered in grated chocolate with mini marshmallows sprinkled on the top. He has decaf coffee and fresh mint tea and I really want for nothing.

Well actually, I do. As the evening passes and we talk, eat, drink and make eye-contact, I find myself wondering if there's the remotest possibility he could satisfy my hunger in the bedroom too.

Sitting together on the sofa, nursing a brandy, I move a little closer to him. He tenses up, then begins to stroke my arm. It takes me a moment to process how this feels. I'm not exactly gagging for him but I don't want to throw up either. I decide to take the initiative. I place my mouth on his and we kiss, dryly, without tongues. I'd rather kiss like this anyway than have a tongue shoved down my throat like corn-mush down a Perigord goose, but there's definitely something missing.

Graymond has a full mouth and has grown a neat goatee that tickles slightly. I picture him going down on me, and subliminally push my hips forward, imagining how it would feel to grind myself against his hard, rough chin, using the friction of his beard to fulfill my needs. I wait for him to pick up my mood, rise up off the sofa and scoop me into his arms. This is his chance to carry me upstairs and ravish me, but he doesn't.

Unfortunately, my fantasy of him turning into Errol Flynn fades like an old fax as he reaches for the Armagnac and pours himself another shot. I realize that nothing more is going to happen tonight, so I stand up, thank him for a lovely evening, gather my things and take my leave. Graymond pecks me warmly on both cheeks and sees me to my car.

I am slightly thrown by the fact that nothing developed after our kiss. I drive home feeling resigned though somewhat confused. There may have been no fireworks of desire, but at least I've avoided any bonfires of despair.

The girls and I get together soon afterwards for our usual catch up. Inevitably, a full post mortem of the date is required and Graymond is dissected on the coroner's table.

'I tried!' I protest when they ask why I didn't give him a go. 'I offered him my virginity but he shoved it back in my face. Shame that was the only thing he shoved in my face! I suspect by the size of his feet that Graymond's got a whopper of a chopper. Fancy not wanting to show that off!'

Three brows try to frown and the third one manages it. (Sensible has an aversion to needles.)

'He must be terrified of you, that's right!' she decides when I've related the story of the aborted kiss. 'What red-blooded male wouldn't have taken it further? He had you on a plate!'

'On a plate, ready and willing to be smeared with melted chocolate and cream,' I agree. 'There was a moment back there when I thought he fancied me and I was all geared up to fancy him back.'

'Of course he fancies you!' Calm says, as if the very notion of his *not* fancying me is absurd. 'You should have taken him in hand, so to speak, not waited for a gilt-edged invitation. I agree with Sensible. He's scared witless. Imagine having to compete with a back catalogue of a thousand toyboys!'

'How *dare* you!' I exclaim. 'It was *two* thousand actually . . .'

'This is how to handle him,' Sensible goes on. 'You invite him round for dinner, cook him a delicious home-made meal, then you slip a little blue pill into his pudding and away you go.'

'I'm not doing that!' I exclaim. 'It'd be like date rape. And do I really want someone who needs Viagra?' I pause, recollecting a fond memory. 'I've only used it once, as an experiment with a toyboy. We took half each, but he was stiff as a truncheon *all* the time anyway so I never knew if it really worked.'

'You're ruined, that's what you are,' says Blondie. 'You've spoilt yourself for anyone else.'

'And he did seem so perfect for you, that's right!' says Sensible, shaking her head despairingly that yet another 'maybe' had turned into a 'maybe not'.

'Maybe you're not his type,' says Half Empty as if reading our thoughts. 'He'd definitely have tried it on if you were.'

She could be right. Maybe Graymond just wants a non-committal, non-addictive, non-sexual relationship. However to keep my homies happy, I agree to have one more crack at it and promise to invite him over soon. Without the Viagra Crumble and Custard.

I'm true to my word and invite Graymond round for dinner the following week. He arrives on time with a bottle of Marqués de Duero and a white orchid in a glass vase. For someone who may not be interested, he certainly comes bearing classy gifts. I offer him a homemade dip with vegetable crisps, he opens the vino and we toast each other's health. A *filet de boeuf en croute* is glistening in the oven and I've laid the table in the dining room with the best linen, china, crystal and cutlery. Ella Fitzgerald warbles on the stereo, *I'll take Manhattan, The Bronx and Staten Island too* . . . At this point, I'll take whatever I can get.

He keeps me company in the kitchen as I prepare the dinner then he follows me into the dining room like a faithful hound, talking about this and that, refilling my glass at ever-increasing intervals.

After we've eaten we move towards the settee. Fuelled by the wine, I decide to instigate the next move. I put a different CD on and before he can sit down, I slide into his arms to dance. He foxtrots me expertly round the coffee table and when the next track begins, we slow the tempo down and I rest my head affectionately on his shoulder. I feel him stiffen – in all the wrong places – but I remind myself that *she who hesitates is lost*.

'Would you like to come and see my etchings?' I ask ingenuously. Graymond gives a nervous whinny, then nods. I take his hand and lead him down the corridor. When we get to my bedroom, I light a scented candle and an incense stick and roll my iPod to an album entitled *Classics for Lovers*. I turn to face Graymond who remains rigid on the threshold to my room.

I smile coquettishly and beckon him towards me, the long red nail of my index finger tickling the air between us. He looks like he's going to pass a kidney stone and comes out with the only line available to him in the circumstances.

'M-Mrs Robinson!' he stammers. 'Are you t-trying to seduce me?'

My throaty chuckle diffuses the tension between us and I take a step forward and begin to undo the buttons of his shirt, deploying all my filmic fantasies to make this scene work for me as well as for him.

I do not find this seduction easy – a thousand 'what ifs' rush through my mind and I can see it all going fantastically wrong.

But then Graymond suddenly experiences a surge of testosterone and pushes me backwards onto the bed, tugs down my panties and dives his face between my legs. Maybe he was so embarrassed he couldn't think of anywhere else to put it; but as his cow-like tongue goes to work and the goatee comes in as handy as I thought it would, I stop worrying.

That is until Graymond fumbles his flies undone and attempts to squeeze his semi-erect penis inside me. It is of considerable girth but I feel it softening as he prods and pushes, and it returns to base camp before he manages to mount any substantial attack.

We're too far gone to back out now, so I tease the Honourable Member up to standing and Graymond climbs aboard, huffing and puffing like Thomas the Tank Engine. He comes surprisingly quickly then slumps off me onto the mattress.

'I'll have to buy shares in Pfizer!' he jokes. A shudder runs through me. Is this the future of my sex life?

'That's was nice,' he yawns as he settles down to sleep. 'And unexpected!'

I don't need to answer as he wouldn't have heard me anyway. He's already snoring.

I lie awake thinking for a very long time.

Graymond and I slide into a comfortable coupledom. I realize quickly that abandoned passion will never blaze between us – the dynamic simply isn't there – but many other good things are: he's a suitable older man; he's kind and considerate and comfortable; and he'll be there today, tomorrow and the next day. He's my Daily Male – the one I can rely on, the one everyone wants me to be with.

There is also a sense of relief at not having to worry about random dating any more. And my being in a secure relationship seems to make a lot of people happy. If I begin to complain about the slightest hint of Grayness in my life I'm told firmly that, 'You can't have your cake and eat it'.

However the fact that I'm eating a lot more cake than I used to indicates a lack of something.

And it's not cake.

One day, I'm out with Blondie. We've decided to meet for tea at Raoul's in Little Venice and I'm tucking into a slice of strudel, which I plan to follow with a chocolate brownie chaser. I'm hardly listening to her conversation as I fulfill my hunger but not my needs. I suddenly catch sight of my chomping gob in the mirror and throw my fork down in disgust, knocking over the teapot in the process.

'Fuck!' I say, angrily.

Blondie smiles sweetly, rights the teapot, summons a waiter, sends away the tea things and orders two glasses of champagne. Then she looks at me and waits.

'I'm sorry darling, but I'm feeling a bit tetchy today,' I confide, as if that wasn't bloody obvious.

'Houston, we have a problem?' she asks.

'Graymond,' I say. 'Rises and falls. Like the Roman Empire, only far, far quicker.'

'You can't have your cake – '

'Yes! So you all keep saying!' I mop up some crumbs from my plate with the ball of my thumb. 'But I don't want any more cake!' I complain. 'I just want a nice hard fuck! Is that too much to ask?'

'It's his age,' she states sorrowfully.

'Yes! I know! And I'm in the same boat as him there. But at least I can still function. I thought Viagra was meant to be failsafe but it doesn't always work. Apparently they have to be "turned on" as well. I'd have hoped he'd be turned on at the very thought of me! My toyboys – '

'They were 40 years younger, darling,' interrupts Blondie, ever the pragmatist.

'Don't I know it!' I reply. 'For some reason, Gray seems to think the only way to give a woman pleasure is by full penetration and if he can't do that, he doesn't do anything! To be quite frank with you,' I go on miserably, 'I'm not sure what I've got myself into.'

Blondie sips her champagne thoughtfully. 'I'm not surprised,' she says at length. 'I've been waiting for this. Your eyes have lost their sparkle you know. What made you think you'd be happy with The Buddha of Suburbia? Same as me trying to settle for Senior Citizen Kane.'

Having neither the courage nor the inclination to finish with Graymond (in exchange for what?), I suggest an invigorating day by the seaside. I've never been to Birchington before and when we get there, I find out why. We park the car on the front, take the hamper I've prepared and begin to walk. It's blowing a gale – well, it is July – and we're obliged to dodge the rising tide and crashing waves by taking refuge in a bus shelter. It begins to rain. Graymond take a gray pac-a-mac out of his pocket and puts it on with the hood done up. He looks like Eeyore on his summer holidays. I'm huddled against the wind with my shawl around my shoulders feeling like Widow Twankey only not as young. The storm picks up in earnest. I remove the thermos from the hamper and pour us two cups of warming tea. Graymond removes *The Economist* from his pocket and begins to read the title page.

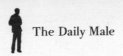

The camera in my mind pulls back and observes us from a distance: a middle-aged couple on a day trip to the coast. In age and intellect, we may match. In every other way, I want to scream.

That night, as I return to his living room after clearing up the dinner things, Graymond lays down his newspaper and says, 'I've got something to ask you.'

I gulp noisily followed by a spluttering fit.

'Oh dear,' I cough, fanning my face with my hand. 'Something must have gone down the wrong way . . . '

If only!

'I've got an investment bond maturing soon,' he says ignoring my discomfort. 'I'll have a bit of disposable income. I want to spend it on the house and I wondered if you'd like to help me. You could . . . ' he goes on more hesitantly, 'move in once it's done.'

My reaction is two-fold: I gush enthusiastically at the thought of chucking out the chintz but stall when I answer the moving-in question.

'You don't need to decide right now,' he says matter-of-factly.

'Thank you for asking,' I answer. 'It is a big decision. But with the new baby and everything . . . I'll think about it, if I may . . . '

I can see it makes sense, and I probably should say 'Yes'. I could rent out my flat and help the kids from the income. Yet something doesn't feel right. Letting my membership to toyboywarehouse. com lapse was sacrifice enough. Can I really turn my back on my old life, my bolt-hole and more especially, my freedom?

What *do* I want, exactly?

Twenty-Seven

I take Graymond up on his offer to help renovate his house but I turn down the invitation to move in with him. It's just too much, too soon and it wouldn't really suit me. I'm eager to set about the refurbishments, though, and waste no time donating the faded fixtures and fittings to charity, putting the old furniture into auction, and generally getting the place spruced up.

Graymond is semi-retired but keeps an office in Marylebone to which he retreats for a few hours each day to piddle about with his portfolio and meet colleagues for lunch. I'm often at his house on my own dealing with the builders, in the multi-faceted role of girlfriend-come-housekeeper-come-interior-decorator. It's an unpaid job, but so is that of 'wife'.

One afternoon, once the house is looking smarter, I'm preparing a dinner party for mutual friends in his streamlined new kitchen, when I look out over the cabbage-patch garden and decide it's time to deal with that. I scroll through yell.com and come across a local landscaper. Justin Thyme: the name makes me smile. I give him a call and we arrange to meet the following morning to discuss what to do with the outside space.

♀

The next day a white pick-up truck draws up and out steps a young man wearing a Stetson hat and a pair of well-worn leather trousers tucked into knee-high boots. A linen shirt cinched in at the waist with a wide belt and a waistcoat complete the outfit.

I open the front door and welcome him through. He's tall and broad with dark, smouldering eyes – someone I'd have made a play for back in the day. He removes his hat and out tumbles a shoulder-length mane of curly black hair. I swallow a gasp. His tanned skin and square jaw are so striking, I feel like I've come face to face with a Cherokee chief.

'Hi!' I say, trying to keep my composure as I stick out my hand for him to shake.

He looks at his own disapprovingly. It's rather grubby with earth beneath the fingernails but he shrugs apologetically, runs it down his trouser leg and shakes mine with a powerful grip. He follows me through the house and into the garden and lets out a whoop when he sees the overgrown space.

'Perfect!' he declares with a southern Irish lilt. 'We'll raze the lot and make a paradise.' And he pulls out a notepad and begins to sketch.

Over the next few weeks, Justin calls round several times and we refine the garden plan. We make a change here, add a feature there, creating an idyll where once there was none. Planting a little Eden in an untamed jungle excites me, and although I try to involve Graymond, he leaves it all to me.

In the evenings, Gray and I dine with friends or listen to music, watch TV and read. I feel secure and safe, but my life is somehow lacking in colour. In fact, I think the Gray-ness is starting to rub off. I've noticed he's put on a bit of weight recently and on the odd occasions when he's on top of me he almost crushes my petite frame. He isn't always pleasant to be close to either, no matter how many zingy toothpastes and anti-perspirants I subtly place on his bathroom shelf.

Although I've suggested he have a pedicure to pumice the scaly skin off his feet, he refuses. 'That sort of thing's for Nancy boys!' he declares.

I think that false machismo is generational. My toyboys never smelled musty, like they'd been left in a drawer for too long. They always seemed so fresh to me, like newly picked fruit. I loved it when they came to me clean-shaven down below, their scrota tight and smooth and silky, not hanging down in folds like the curtains I threw out. I remember the bulging muscles of their arms, the outlined definition of their pecs, the sinews in their thighs, their well-toned satin backs, their butt-cheeks firm as footballs in the palms of both my hands . . .

I have to turn away when Gray gets out of bed to cross the room, his baggy balls and blancmange buttocks wobbling as he walks. And then I feel guilty because it's not his fault. My body's softer too. And Graymond is good to me, generous and caring, and I know I shouldn't question it if this is not enough. The greatest tragedy of growing old is that everything ages except your feelings.

One morning, Justin and I set off to a specialist garden centre to explore the darkest reaches of the vast, glass greenhouses. We creep through the undergrowth like intrepid explorers in search of lost varieties of exotic flora. I have a fantasy moment as I imagine travelling with him to the denser forests of South America in search of lost species, living off the fruits of the land, cooking fish from the rivers, lying beneath the stars beside a crackling fire. The clipped wings on my back twitch a little and begin to flap.

Heading back to London listening to his music, my senses respond to being close to him. There's such a virile quality about this man: he's so earthy, so potent. My nipples start to tingle and I find myself inhaling him. I tell myself to stop. My life is very different now and I shouldn't do anything to jeopardize that.

As he navigates the evening traffic, I ask if he'll drive me back to my home. I need to sleep alone tonight. I steal a look at his chiselled profile and the way his legs tense as he shifts up through the gears and I feel that old pull of longing deep inside.

Justin stops the engine outside my flat and turns to look at me.

'Tell me what's wrong with you today?' he asks in his soft, languid way. 'You're not your normal self. You've a wistful expression in your eyes . . .'

I hesitate. What should I say? *I used to love young men like you but I'm not allowed to any more?*

Says who, anyway? And is it as simple as that?

'Come up for coffee,' I declare impetuously and we both get out the truck.

Justin follows me up my stairs like so many men before him. I have a sense of prevailing excitement mixed with anxiety; an anticipation I used to feel that I'm trying now to quell.

I put the kettle on and get the milk out of the fridge and when I turn around, he's standing propped against the counter, arms folded across his chest, cowboy-booted feet crossed at the ankles just watching me. His presence dominates the room, stimulates yet unnerves me. He acts so cool and looks so hot . . . I slam the lid on my next thought.

He says nothing. He doesn't have to. I'm probably exuding the same pheromones as a bitch on heat.

The kettle starts to boil and the steam blows in my hair and he leans over and turns the spout away. His arm is right across me now, brushing my breasts and I just want to push myself against him.

I pull away instead and reach into the cupboard for the coffee. He removes it from my grasp and puts it down firmly on the worktop. Then takes my chin in his hand and turns me round to face him.

'There's a woman round here could use some loving . . . ' he says in his lilting drawl.

I laugh nervously. The sound slices through the tension in the air. 'Raymond loves me,' I answer, more to myself than to him.

'But not the way I can,' is his simple answer.

He surprises me then by lifting me effortlessly onto the counter. I feel very vulnerable with him standing hard up to me, pinning me to where I sit. He picks up a lock of my hair and tucks it tenderly behind my ear then lowers his mouth onto mine and parts my lips with his tongue, igniting a fire that flares too fast.

A fierce, demanding energy takes hold of me and I rake my fingers through his mane and hold him fast as I kiss him back with all my might. He runs his hands up both my thighs but I come to my senses suddenly and stop him.

'What are you doing?' I ask angrily, more at myself than him.

'Isn't this what you need?' he replies. 'What you want?'

'Yes . . . NO! I don't know . . . '

I quench the craving erupting inside me and jump off the worktop. I open the cupboard and crash the cups down from the shelf.

'Milk and sugar?' I bark, hoping to stabilize the situation with kitchen normality.

My heart is beating too fast. I was losing myself in the depths of him, the roughness of his beard against my skin, his body hard and forceful as he pressed himself . . .

I pick up the kettle and quiver the boiling water into the cups. It splashes everywhere. He just stands there looking at me.

'What?' I ask aggressively.

'You,' he answers.

'What about me?'

'You're living someone else's life.'

'That's my business!' I argue. 'Please drink your coffee then I want you to go!'

He turns on his stacked heel and walks out the door. I stand there shaking, annoyed that some . . . some *gardener* found it so easy to steal the paddle from my canoe.

And yet that kiss . . .

I know I must take stock again. I don't call any girlfriends. This is one stock-take I have to do alone. I snatch my keys up off the desk and go for a long walk across the park. I sit down on a bench and stare out at the landscape.

I could just erase the moment with Justin as if it never happened and continue with Graymond, couldn't I? He really doesn't need to know. And I'm a good enough actress to fake it – but do I really want that? I know my future's safe with him, but maybe this is a future for me at 72 not 62. It seems there are too many unlit fireworks in the Wendy Warehouse to close it down just yet.

And through this mental argument, one enduring theme returns: if it isn't to be Justin, it will eventually be somebody else.

I know I'm calmer now. After my trip to Ecuador I feel more comfortable in my skin, with just being me. So do I really need a man around? Do I need to compromise, settle down with someone I'm not sure about, just for the sake of 'society', just for the sake of 'it'? Is that fair on me – and is it fair on him?

And am I trying to live someone else's life?

With that, the decision is made. If I end up alone, as I'm certain that I must, at least I'll know *I* made that choice. I'm being true to myself and, in so doing, being true to the people around me.

The Sisterhood, with the exception of Blondie, declares me insane.

The man in question, meanwhile, cannot understand what he'd done wrong.

I use an old cliché but it's the truth. 'It's not you, it's me,' I say. I go on to explain, as kindly as I can, that I was feeling stifled and that he deserved more than that.

Finally he asks if there was someone else.

I answer as truthfully as I can. 'Not really . . . but in time there may have been.'

Like the perfect gentleman he is, Graymond thanks me for my honesty, painful as it is. He suggests, generously, that we remain friends. He tells me he would miss me otherwise and I readily agree: I fear I'll miss him too.

And so I take my toothbrush and make-up out of his spanking new bathroom cabinet, stick them in my handbag and go on my way. Not without a tear, I must confess, for it is daunting giving up this stability to dive once more into the shark-infested waters of the singles social scene.

I'm just a little frightened but I feel really, truly alive.

♀

I'm alone again, but not for long, because then something truly miraculous happens. A new boy enters my life . . . maybe the only boy I'll ever need again.

Monday 9 p.m. Lily is in labour! At last! I rush over and drive the expectant parents to the hospital. The baby's already nine days late and they've both been getting impatient and upset. Her labour has started and stopped twice but now, at last, things begin to happen.

I pace the corridor where I'm not supposed to be and post myself outside her room. I push the door open a crack so I can see what's going on. At one point a paediatrician pushes past and goes inside and I pray, *Oh Lord*, I pray . . .

As I sense the tempo hotting up I crane my neck to see beyond the chaos. The atmosphere is super-charged in there, the midwife and nurses around the bed all shouting, 'Come on Lily . . . Push! Push!'

My eyes spill over and I clutch my chest as I watch my baby try to bring *her* baby into the world. After a heart-stopping moment, a little blue head emerges and stays there way too long before its slippery blue body follows. It has boy bits between its chubby legs and once it (he!) starts to cry, he turns pink then red and everybody's smiles and says: 'Congratulations! You have a son!'

I run down the corridor into the arms of my second ex-husband, Lily's Dad, and then the in-laws arrive and we all hug and kiss each other in excitement and relief.

Then I rush back to wait outside Lily's room and watch my poor daughter being stitched up. There is carnage all around I don't wish to describe, but her handsome young husband is

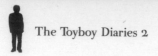

standing by the window transfixed, his brand new son coddled safely in his arms, an expression of adoration and wonderment in his wide blue eyes.

When Lily is comfortable and returned to dignity, the family is allowed in. The heavens open and it begins to pour. They tell us proudly the baby is to be called Noah. When I lift him up and give him his first kiss, I know I'll never love another boy so much as long as I live.*

*I might have to rescind this. A few months later, Poppy becomes pregnant again. At the time of going to press, we don't know what sex it is! Either way, I know I'll adore it just as much – how could I not? I'm its groovy grandma!

Afterglow

The next few days are a bit of a blur. Lily is discharged from hospital but returns a total of seven times for various queries and complications. Life is put on hold as everything revolves around the little man cub and tending to his every need.

As Lily recovers, she decides to return to college to qualify as a Naturopath. I step in to help look after Noah one full day each week. I have to re-learn how to change a nappy, make a bottle, bring up wind, fold and unfold a pushchair, get him in and out of the car seat, bathe him without drowning the tiny mite and generally keep the little cherub happy from eight thirty till half past six. It's a tough job but I love every minute of it.

I learn never to make plans for the evenings of a Noah day – I can barely stand, let alone articulate. Much like any other little boy, he works me hard and makes me smile – and leaves me totally exhausted.

One day, a shop assistant leans over the pram to admire him and says, 'You look just like your Mummy,' and I proudly answer, 'He's gorgeous isn't he? But he's my grandson!'

Graymond and I keep in touch and when I inform him about the new arrival he takes me out to 'wet the baby's head.'

While we're clinking glasses and ordering a meal, he teases me about the incomplete state of his garden.

'Oh . . . ' I say blushing, and stammer out an apology. 'I could try to get that finished for you, if you'd like?'

'Save me the job!' he booms. 'I've only ever grown a beard and that wasn't very successful either.'

Oh Gray . . . you had a narrow escape, I think to myself.

Later that evening, I spend some time pacing and staring at the phone. It reminds me of MLP and when I had The Damp Patch. Eventually I pluck up the courage and make the call.

'Justin Thyme,' comes the lilting Irish voice and I feel myself quiver.

'Hi Justin,' I say nervously. 'It's . . . er . . . Wendy here. I was wondering whether you were available to come back and finish the job?'

'What job would that be now?' he asks sardonically and I can't help but laugh.

'The green one!' I reply. 'The Garden of Eden?'

'Ah! *That* unfinished job.' he comments. 'I was hoping you meant the other one . . . '

'Well . . . ' I say.

At 9 p.m. my doorbell rings. Just in time . . . But that's another story.

The End

Acknowledgements

Without the faith, friendship and encouragement of my Super Agent, Adrian Weston of RAFT PR, and the enthusiasm shown by the team at Old Street Publishing, the blog that became this book would have remained in cyberspace.

A special mention must go to my editor, Becky Senior, who carved my random ramblings into bite-size pieces and presented me with the ingredients for a 27-course meal. All I had to do was cook it!

My enduring, unswerving and most heartfelt thanks must go, as ever, to the Sisterhood – my 'Tiller Girls' and much-loved support system, who continue to steer me vicariously through still waters and storms. Omnipotent and omni-present, they are here for me – as I am for them – through thick and thin (be they thighs or otherwise).

Adrianne: calm, composed and cool in any crisis, who knew the characters involved and never once said, 'Are you completely mad?!'

Bernice: the voice of reason and good sense.

Frances: whether she be here, there or anywhere.

Julia: for founding toyboywarehouse.com, a great source of material!

Karen: always available with a caring shoulder – even when it was frozen.

Maggi: juicy Plum, earth mother and mind goddess.

Marilyn: my wonderful sister – the saint by the seaside – who puts everyone else's needs before her own.

Michele: for her morning calls, dry wit, patient ear and superb suggestions when I was so edited-out, I no longer knew how to spell the word 'dog'.

My lovely Buddies: especially Gerry, Michael, Peter, Richard (aka Toby Kell-Ogg), Sue and Steven, who accept my vagaries and give good counsel.

And last but not least, I thank my children, Gabrielle and Lauren, for putting up with my occasional unavailability while I was 'doing the research' . . . and for providing me with the true loves of my life – my darling grandchildren.

I thank you all so very much.